SAM WALTON　　MAHATMA GANDHI　　WALT DISNEY

8 ATTRIBUTES *of* GREAT ACHIEVERS

CAMERON C. TAYLOR

ORVILLE WRIGHT　　ABRAHAM LINCOLN　　WARREN BUFFETT

BENJAMIN FRANKLIN　　WINSTON CHURCHILL　　GEORGE WASHINGTON

TREMENDOUS LIFE BOOKS.com

This book is a work of:

Does Your Bag Have Holes? Foundation.
428 E. Thunderbird Road #504, Phoenix, AZ 85022
Phone: 1-877-No-Holes (664-6537) Fax: 1-480-393-4432
CustomerService@DoesYourBagHaveHoles.org
http://www.DoesYourBagHaveHoles.org

ISBN-13: 978-1-933715-89-6

Printed in the United States of America

To my wife, Paula, for her energetic spirit, loving support, and eternal friendship. I am blessed to have such a wonderful companion.

TABLE OF CONTENTS

Attribute 8: Persistent

Conclusion

Endnotes

Illustration Credits

About the Author

INTRODUCTION

As I have studied the lives of hundreds of great achievers, I have found that they each have possessed or currently possess certain attributes that were foundational to their achievements. Sometimes we see those who have achieved great success and think they are somehow uniquely gifted or talented and that we could never duplicate their success; however, great achievers are not simply born, they are developed. Each great achiever has worked to develop attributes throughout their life. For example, as a young man, Washington copied out in his own handwriting the code of a moral life and strived to live by it.[1]

Benjamin Franklin recorded in his autobiography the desire to possess thirteen virtues. He then described the process of reviewing and working to develop each of these virtues, writing, "My intention being to acquire the habitude of all these virtues, I judged it would be well not to distract my attention by attempting the whole at once, but to fix one of them at a time . . . I made a little book, in which I allotted a page for each of the virtues. I ruled each page with red ink, so as to have seven columns, one for each day of the week, marking each column with a letter for the day. I crossed these columns with thirteen red lines, marking the beginning of each line with the first letter of one of the virtues, on which line, and in its proper column, I might mark, by a little black spot, every fault I found upon examination to have been committed respecting that virtue upon that day. I determined to give a week's strict attention to each of the virtues successively. Thus, in the first week, my great guard was to avoid the least offence against Temperance, leaving the other virtues to their ordinary chance, only marking every evening the faults of the day. Thus, if in the first week I could keep my first line, marked T, clear of spots, I supposed the habit of that virtue so much strengthened and its opposite weakened that I might venture extending my attention to include the next, and for the following week keep both lines clear of spots. Proceeding thus to the last, I could go through a course complete in thirteen weeks, and four courses in a year. And like him who, having a garden to weed, does not attempt to eradicate all the bad herbs at once, which would exceed his reach and his strength, but works on one of the beds at a time, and, having accomplished the first, proceeds to a second, so I should have, I hoped, the encouraging pleasure of seeing on my pages the progress I made in virtue."[2]

This book will help you develop the character attributes that lead to greater achievement. In determining what makes organizations great, Jim Collins, author of *Good to Great*, discovered that the "good-to-great companies placed greater weight on character attributes than on specific educational background, practical skills, specialized knowledge or work experience."[3]

Working to perfect the 8 character attributes discussed in this book will help you achieve sustained, superior performance by helping you develop your most valuable resource—you.

ATTRIBUTE 1: RESPONSIBLE

"The price of greatness is responsibility."

– Winston Churchill

CHAPTER I

CHOICE AND CONSEQUENCE

"Every choice carries a consequence. For better or worse, each choice is the unavoidable consequence of its predecessor. There are not exceptions. If you can accept that a bad choice carries the seed of its own punishment, why not accept the fact that a good choice yields desirable fruit?"
– Gary Ryan Blair

Every time we make a choice, we are either obeying or disobeying a law of success. As we obey the laws of success, we move to a more successful state of happiness, peace, power, freedom, and prosperity. As we disobey the laws of success, we move to a state of sadness, weakness, bondage, and misery. Each moment we are progressing toward one of these two states. This gift of choice is like fire: if properly used, it can create warmth and life; if improperly used, it can burn or even kill.

With each choice comes a consequence. No amount of rationalizing or complaining will alter the consequence. If you pick up one end of a stick (choice), you also pick up the other end of the stick (consequence of that choice).

Farm Metaphor

On a farm, you reap what you sow. If you plant corn, you harvest corn. You cannot plant corn and harvest watermelon. Similarly, we reap what we sow in life. Our choices are the seeds and the consequences are the harvest. At times, we may attempt to choose the consequences of our choices or misunderstand what the consequence of a choice will be. We might want to eat 10,000 calories a day, but not gain weight. We might want to smoke cigarettes, but not get lung cancer. We might want to disobey laws of success, but still have freedom and prosperity. This is as foolish as a farmer planting corn and expecting to harvest watermelon. Some might also expect financial abundance but learn nothing regarding the laws of wealth. This is as silly as a farmer not planting and expecting a great harvest.

There is a human desire to be miraculously delivered from the consequences of an action. We tend to seek a rescue from consequences with little or no effort on our part. This tendency can easily be seen manifested by those who have incurred large amounts of debt and then seek to be delivered from the bondage and obligation of repayment through bankruptcy, or those who seek deliverance from a disease of choice by taking a pill to treat the symptoms instead of changing the behavior that causes the symptoms. We should seek to change our actions because we cannot choose the consequences. We must accept responsibility, which is the willingness and ability to recognize and accept the consequences of our actions.

Number of Choices Paradox

We have all heard someone describe freedom as, "No one can tell me what to do. I am in charge of my own life. To be free one must not be bound by laws." The laws of success are not restrictive, but are a road map to joy. The violation of these laws is not freedom, but bondage, pain, and misery. Those who know and live the laws of success enjoy freedom, joy, and prosperity. Thus, obedience to the laws of success brings freedom.

The correct use of our power to choose will result in more choices. The misuse will result in fewer choices. Each time we make a choice, we either gain more freedom as a result of our increased choices or digress toward bondage as the result of our diminished choices.

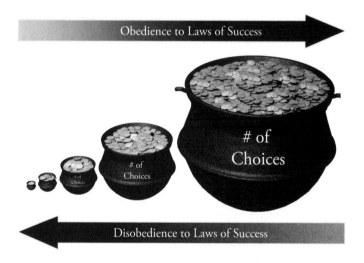

Bank Metaphor

"If someone decides to rob a bank, for instance, he or she may be incarcerated under the law. That person not only lost the ability to rob banks, but is also restricted from other lawful activities in the future. A trip to the park, while lawful, is no longer an option after incarceration. The opposite is also true. If one chooses to open a bank and work hard within the boundaries of the law, they can continue that activity and will have opportunities that they did not have previously. A lawful and successful enterprise would provide funding for additional activities that the person could not afford before their choice to provide banking services."[4]

Prison Lecture

While speaking at a prison to a group of the inmates,[5] I asked for a volunteer from the inmates to describe his dream life. After a long pause and some prodding, one of the inmates began to speak. I was rather surprised by his vivid description of a successful career, a beautiful home, and a happy family.

I then asked, "Why are you in prison?"

The inmate responded, "For drugs."

I then asked if drugs would take him away from or toward the dream life he described. I will never forget his response, "I can have both."

I replied by saying, "What would happen if you touched a hot stove with your bare hand?"

The inmate replied, "I would get burned."

I continued, "What if you don't want to get burned? Can you just choose to touch a hot stove and not get burned?" He, of course, answered no.

I then taught that we can choose whether or not to touch a hot stove, but we cannot decide whether or not we get burned. We can choose our actions, but we cannot choose the consequences of our choices. Getting burned is a natural consequence of touching a hot stove just like a prison sentence is the consequence of being involved with illegal drugs.

To this the inmate replied, "I am in prison, have no money,

am divorced, and rarely see my kids. If you're so smart, how do I change this?"

I answered, "You need to learn and live the laws of success."

The inmate replied, "What do you mean?"

I continued, "Our lives are governed by laws, such as gravity. A child, though ignorant of the law, will still fall if he jumps off a ledge. The laws that govern wealth, health, and relationships are as clear and as binding as those that govern the earth, such as gravity. Regardless of whether or not we know or understand the laws, they always operate the same. Our success or failure, our happiness or unhappiness, depends on our knowledge and application of these laws in our lives."

The inmate then asked, "So why are some people rich and some poor?"

I replied, "Why are some people physically fit and others overweight?" I explained that people's health differs because they have made different choices. Consider someone with a lot of money, but is also overweight. This person has learned to live financial laws but does not live the health laws. Something similar could be said about someone who is in great shape, but is also poor. They have learned to live the laws of health but not the laws of wealth. The great news is that you can be successful in all areas of your life by living the laws related to each area.

The inmate then asked, "You are obviously successful—can I achieve success?"

In response, I asked the inmate to climb on the table he was sitting at and I climbed onto the table at the front of the room. I then said, "On the count of three, jump off the table. One, two, three." We both jumped off the table and hit the floor. I continued teaching that the law of gravity affected both of us the same regardless of age, gender, race, or upbringing. This is also true of the laws of success. They are the same now as they were in the past and will be the same in the future. Our knowledge about these laws may fluctuate, but their principles and application will never change. Anyone can be successful, because anyone can learn and follow the laws of success.

We all have the power to choose what we will become. All men and women are born equal, but then become unequal as they make decisions. Everyone chooses to obey laws differently. One may choose to play softball while another may choose to build a business. One may choose to turn on the television while another may choose to read a book. One may choose to golf on his day off while another chooses to spend time with family. One may choose to listen to the radio on the way to work while another may choose to listen to audio books. We are born equal, yet years later we live diversely, all because we chose to live laws differently. It is really very simple. Following laws of success results in positive outcomes.

A prison guard then asked, "How much money did you make last year?"

I replied, "How much money did you make last year?"

The guard replied, "$30,000."

I then answered his question by saying, "I made ten times more than you did last year. Do you think I am ten times smarter than you or ten times better than you?"

The guard thought about the question and replied, "No, you are not ten times smarter or better than me."

To make my point clear, I continued, "There is no difference between you and me. I have just learned certain financial principles. There are certain principles for marital success, there are certain principles for spiritual success, and there are certain principles for financial success. If one desires to, one can dramatically increase his or her income by learning and applying the laws of wealth."

Years later, I was at a chamber of commerce meeting and recognized the inmate I had spoken with at the prison. He approached me and said, "Thank you so much for visiting me in prison; your message changed my life. I always wondered why some men had great lives while mine was miserable. I saw people with successful careers, beautiful homes, and happy families and wondered why my life was just the opposite. Once I learned that there were laws of success, my heart was filled with hope and peace. I realized that all I had to do was learn these laws and then have courage, discipline, and the guts to obey them. Once I realized this, I knew that I would one day live in the home of my dreams, have no debt, and be a hero to my wife and children. It has been a long road, but I have transformed my life from one of bondage and misery to one of freedom and prosperity."

CHAPTER II

THE POWER TO CHOOSE

*"The greatest power that a person
possesses is the power to choose."*

– J. Martin Kohe

There are some who believe man is the product of his
environment. Sigmund Freud once asserted, "Let one attempt to
expose a number of the most diverse people uniformly to hunger.
With the increase of the imperative urge of hunger all individual
differences will blur, and in their stead will appear the uniform
expression of the one unstilled urge."[6] Viktor Frankl disputed
this notion. Writing of his experience in Nazi prison camps, Mr.
Frankl declared, "The 'individual differences' did not 'blur' but,
on the contrary, people became more different; people unmasked
themselves, both the swine and the saints."[7] "In the midst of the
most degrading circumstances imaginable, Frankl used the human
endowment of self-awareness to discover a fundamental principle
about the nature of man: Between stimulus and response, man
has the freedom to choose."[8] Those in the prison camp were in a
similar, negative environment, but the people were very different
depending on how they chose to respond and act.

At the conclusion of World War II, the survivors in the
concentration camps were freed. Many prisoners were weak and
filled with anger. In one of the camps, the American soldiers
observed a man who appeared to be strong, happy, and peaceful.

His posture was erect, his eyes bright, his energy unwavering. The soldiers assumed he had recently been imprisoned or had not suffered as the other prisoners had. As this prisoner was questioned, it was learned that "for six years he had lived on the same starvation diet, slept in the same airless and disease-ridden barracks as everyone else, but without the least physical or mental deterioration."[9] Explaining what made the difference, he related the following: "We lived in the Jewish section of Warsaw [capital of Poland], my wife, two daughters, and our three little boys. When the Germans reached our street they lined everyone against a wall and opened up with machine guns. I begged to be allowed to die with my family, but because I spoke German they put me in a work group. I had to decide right then whether to let myself hate the soldiers who had done this. It was an easy decision, really. I was a lawyer. In my practice I had seen too often what hate could do to people's minds and bodies. Hate had just killed the six people who mattered most to me in the world. I decided then that I would spend the rest of my life—whether it was a few days or many years—loving every person I came in contact with."[10]

We have within us the power to choose how we respond to a hurtful situation. We cannot control the actions of others, but we can control how we will respond. As we understand our power to choose, we see that we are in control. Our life is not a result of our environment or upbringing, but a result of our choices. We have the ability to determine the kind of life we want to live and the type of person we wish to be.

Thermostat vs. Thermometer

This idea of choice can be illustrated through an analogy between a thermometer and a thermostat. A thermometer is stationary and only reflects what is happening around it. It simply responds to its environment. If it is hot outside, it reports it is hot. If it is cold outside, it reports it is cold. A thermostat, on the other hand, measures what the temperature is and then responds by changing the temperature to the conditions it desires. If it wants the temperature to be cooler, it turns on the air conditioner and cools the room down. If it wants the temperature to be warmer, it turns on the heater. Some people are like a thermometer. If their environment is negative, they are negative. If bad things happen, they are sad. If good things happen, they are happy. They are simply a product of their environment. Successful people, on the other hand, are more like a thermostat. Even if their environment is negative, they choose to be positive.

Happiness Comes from Within

My grandmother passed away several years ago, and I was asked to speak at her funeral. In my comments, I shared the following: "What qualities did Grandma Taylor radiate throughout her life? She radiated many—strengthening thousands of people—but there are a few qualities that stand paramount in my mind. One was that of happiness. I cannot remember a single encounter with Grandma when she was not happy and positive. Even as her health declined, and though her circumstances were far from ideal, she always maintained a happy, positive attitude. Since she struggled with many physical ailments, such as broken bones and lost memory, it would have been easy and justifiable to have become sad and discouraged, but this was never the case. She continued to strengthen and build those around her. I recall that after visiting, she would often give departing words of encouragement such as, 'Be good.' From this, I have learned the powerful lesson that happiness doesn't depend on outward conditions but on those inside."

The Accidental Gift

My wife, Paula, is one of the most loving, friendly, outgoing people I know. A few years ago she was in a car accident. She was stopped at a traffic light when a person three cars back failed to stop, causing a four-car accident. My wife did not have her insurance information with her. When I arrived with the insurance information, the police were taking statements and information. The drivers of the other damaged cars were upset and angry, but Paula was happy and making friends. Paula went up to the driver responsible for the accident and gave her a hug and said, "You need a present." My wife then gave her two tickets to a local college football game taking place on the upcoming Saturday. The girl said in shock, "I damaged your car and caused you and your baby a great deal of stress, and you're giving me a present?" But as my wife demonstrated, driving can only cause us frustration and anger if we choose to respond that way.

Taking Responsibility

During his career, Hall of Fame quarterback Steve Young threw 203 interceptions, and he threw two interceptions in a row on six occasions. Steve Young commented that after each interception, "The coaches, my teammates, and the fans want an explanation. I could give excuses like 'the receiver ran the wrong route,' 'the lineman missed a block,' 'the ball slipped,' 'I lost my footing.' I found that using excuses was never very effective. I learned to take responsibility for the mistake. When I would throw an interception, I would say, 'I messed up' with no excuses and I would then tell my teammates that we are going to go to the sideline and when we get the ball back we are going to try again. We are going to go back on the field and score a touchdown. My teammates and coaches responded much better when I took responsibility for the mistake than when I looked for someone or something to blame."[11]

Victor Mentality Instead of Victim Mentality

"Since the 1970s several sociologists and social critics have noted the increase in individuals claiming to be victims and then using that status to relieve themselves of responsibility . . . [and] the tendency to use victimization as a justification, excuse, and explanation for wrongful behavior and personal irresponsibility."[12] "Instead of making an effort, some people make excuses for not doing what they could be doing. We hear the argument, 'I was denied the advantages others had in their youth.' Others say, 'I am physically handicapped.' But history is full of examples of people with physical handicaps who went on to greatness. The Greek poet Homer, the English poet John Milton, and the American historian William Prescott, had good excuses—they were blind. Athenian Demosthenes, greatest of all great orators, had a wonderful excuse—his lungs were weak, his voice was hoarse and unmusical, and he stuttered. The great German composer Ludwig van Beethoven continued to compose even after he became totally deaf. They all had good excuses for not doing anything—but they never used those excuses."[13]

Mahatma Gandhi – From Shy Boy to "The Great Soul"

Before Gandhi became the leader of 500 million people who called him "The Mahatma," which means "The Great Soul," and before he became the father of a nation by winning the fight for independence, he was a shy boy and an average man. Gandhi wrote, "I claim to be no more than an average man with below average capabilities. . . I have not the shadow of a doubt that any man or woman can achieve what I have, if he or she would put forth the same effort and cultivate the same hope and faith."

Gandhi was born on October 2, 1869, in Porbandar, India. At the time of his birth, India had been ruled by the English for over 200 years. "There was nothing unusual about the boy Mohandas Karamchand Gandhi, expect perhaps that he was very, very shy. He had no unusual talent, and went through school as a somewhat less than average student."[14] Gandhi wrote of his childhood, "It was with some difficulty that I got through the multiplication tables. . . [and] I used to be very, very shy and avoid all company. . . [I would] run back home as soon as the school closed. . . I literally ran back, because I could not bear to talk to anybody. . . Moreover, I was a coward." Even as a teenager, Gandhi was afraid of the dark and could not bear to sleep without a light in the room.

At age 13, Gandhi married Kasturba Makanji. After high school, Gandhi went to college, but after five months he returned home after failing every class. Gandhi's uncle then suggested that he go to London to study law to become a barrister (lawyer). Gandhi's wife, Kasturba, sold her jewelry to pay for Gandhi's ticket and he headed for London. His first months in England were a great struggle. He wrote of the experience, "At night the tears would stream down my cheeks, and home memories made sleep out of the question. It was impossible to share my misery with anyone. I knew of nothing that would soothe me. Everything was strange." "For weeks Gandhi was on the verge of turning back and taking the next boat home. But . . . something deeper within him was determined to stick it out."[15]

In 1891 at age 21, after three years in London, Gandhi returned to India to practice law. "He was an immediate failure. Not only did he not know how to apply legal principles to particular situations, his English book-learning left him without the slightest knowledge of Indian law. No one would dream of giving him a case. . . His colleagues began to refer to him laughingly as the 'briefless barrister'. . . His first case . . . was a routine, ten-dollar claim. Gandhi stood up with trembling knees to make his cross examination, but discovered abruptly that he could not utter a single word. Finally, amidst his colleagues' laughter, he handed the case over to someone with more experience and fled the room."[16]

At this point, Gandhi's brother had found an opportunity for Gandhi to work in South Africa doing minor clerical work. Gandhi was happy to have a job and hoped it would provide him with some good experience. This job turned out to be more complicated than Gandhi anticipated, however. His job was to advise the legal counsel for a business that was inept at keeping accurate accounting records. Gandhi had no background in accounting, so the task before him was a daunting one. In the past Gandhi retreated when faced with difficult situations.

Gandhi began to realize, though, that life seemed to have an endless amount of challenges, and as soon as he ran away from one problem, another one would appear in a new circumstance. Gandhi knew that what needed to be changed were not his circumstances but himself, and this time he was going to have the courage to make those personal changes. Gandhi immersed himself in his work. He studied bookkeeping. He examined every detail of the case to uncover the truth. Soon Gandhi understood the case better than anyone involved on either side of the dispute. Although his client had a strong case, the legal process could be drawn out for a long period of time. If this happened, the only individuals to benefit from the situation would be the attorneys, and Gandhi wasn't interested in making a profit at his client's expense.

Gandhi was able to convince both sides to settle out of court using the arbitration process. The opponents were relatives, so Gandhi was interested in settling the issue quickly to prevent further damage to the relationship. It took a lot of work by Gandhi in the arbitration to reconcile the parties, but in the end both sides were satisfied. Gandhi wrote of the experience, "I had learnt the true practice of law. I had learnt to find out the better side of human nature and to enter men's hearts. I realized that the true function of a lawyer was to unite parties riven asunder." His experience working in the South African law firm taught him that success came by changing himself, not by changing his environment.

This was the beginning of Gandhi's success as an attorney. His focus on service and reconciliation began to win the trust of many clients and helped him build a successful law practice. Gandhi also began what he called "my experiment with truth." He began studying various sources of truth and applying and testing the teachings in his own life. Gandhi said of the truths he strived to live by: "I have nothing new to teach the world. Truth and nonviolence are as old as the hills. . . Those who believe in the simple truths I have laid down can propagate them only by living them."

Truth 1: *"Be the change you want to see in the world."* -Gandhi

"A mother once brought her child to [Gandhi], asking him to tell the young boy not to eat sugar, because it was not good for his diet or his developing teeth. Gandhi replied, 'I cannot tell him that. But you may bring him back in a month.' The mother was frustrated as . . . she had traveled some distance, and had expected the great leader to support her parenting. . . Four weeks later she returned, not sure what to expect. The great Gandhi took the small child's hand into his own, knelt before him, and tenderly cautioned, 'Do not eat sugar, my child. It is not good for you.' Then he embraced him and returned the boy to his mother. The mother, grateful but perplexed, queried, 'Why didn't you say that a month ago?' 'Well,' said Gandhi, 'a month ago, I was still eating sugar.'"[17] Gandhi knew that to effectively lead others he must first lead himself. Gandhi wrote, "How can I control others if I cannot control myself?"

On another occasion "Gandhi was on a train pulling out of the station, [and] a European reporter running alongside his compartment asked him, 'Do you have a message I can take back to my people?' It was a day of silence for Gandhi, part of his regular practice, so he didn't reply. Instead he scribbled a few words on a piece of paper and passed it to the journalists: 'My life is my message.'"[18] Gandhi believed that "an ounce of practice is worth more than tons of preaching."[19]

Truth 2: *"Nobody can hurt me without my permission."* -Gandhi

"As Gandhi hurriedly boarded a train that was beginning to depart, one of his sandals fell onto the tracks, and he immediately responded by taking off his second sandal and throwing it onto the tracks, so that later somebody would find both sandals and have a pair to wear."[20] Gandhi turned the negative experience of losing his sandal into a positive opportunity for service and giving. Gandhi believed that "experience is not what happens to you; it is what you do with what happens to you."[21]

"H.G. Wells once asked for Gandhi's views on a document Wells had co-authored entitled 'Rights of Man.' Gandhi did not agree with the document's emphasis on rights. He responded with a cable that said, 'I suggest the right way. Begin with a charter of Duties of Man and I promise the rights will follow as spring follows winter."[22]

Gandhi wrote of the harsh treatment, imprisonment, and oppression he received, "You can chain me, you can torture me, you can even destroy this body, but you will never imprison my mind. . . The moment the slave resolves that he will no longer be a slave his fetters fall. . . freedom and slavery are mental states. . . They cannot take away our self-respect if we do not give it to them."

Truth 3: *"It is easy enough to be friendly to one's friends. But to befriend the one who regards himself as your enemy is the quintessence of true religion."* -Gandhi

Gandhi fought for equal rights, fair treatment, and independence from British domination for the Indian people, but his was not the traditional fight. Gandhi sought to overcome their exploitation "by returning love for hatred, and respect for contempt."[23] Gandhi had learned, "When one person hates another, it is the hater who falls ill—physically, emotionally, spiritually. When he loves, it is he who becomes whole. Hatred kills. Love heals."[24] He also discovered that "an eye for eye only ends up making the whole world blind."[25] Gandhi challenged the people, "Do not resort to violence even if it seems at first to promise success; it can only contradict your purpose. Use the means of love and respect even if the result seems far off or uncertain. . . If we can adhere [to these principles], India's freedom is assured. . . I hold myself to be incapable of hating any being on earth. . . But I can and do hate evil wherever it exists. I hate the system of government that the British people have set up in India. I hate the ruthless exploitation of India. . . I do not hate the domineering Englishmen. . . I seek to reform them in all the loving ways that are open to me. My noncooperation has its roots not in hatred, but in love. . ."[26]

When scholar J.B. Kripalani first heard Gandhi talk about fighting for independence with love and respect instead of violence, he walked up to Gandhi and told him, "Mr. Gandhi . . . you know nothing at all about history. Never has a nation been able to free itself without violence." Gandhi smiled and replied, "You know nothing about history. The first thing you have to learn about history is that because something has not taken place in the past that does not mean it cannot take place in the future."[27]

As a result of Gandhi's refusal to obey unjust laws, he was imprisoned several times, spending six and a half years of his life in prison. During one of his stays in prison he made a pair of sandals for the man responsible for his imprisonment, Field General Jan Smuts. Many years later Smuts wrote of Gandhi: "In jail he prepared for me a pair of sandals. I have worn them for many a summer, though I feel that I am not worthy to stand in the shoes of so great a man."[28] Late in his life Gandhi said of General Smuts, "He started with being my bitterest opponent and critic. Today he is my warmest friend."

The Great Soul

"Gandhi never held any official position in government, he had no wealth, he commanded no armies—but he could mobilize millions."[29] As a result of his example and personal character, millions organized together to fight to become a self-reliant and independent nation. On August 15, 1947, after decades of effort, the goal was achieved. Jawaharlal Nehru, first prime minister of India, said in a speech on the eve of independence, "On this day our first thoughts go to the architect of this freedom, the Father of our Nation [Gandhi], who . . . held aloft the torch of freedom and lighted up the darkness that surrounded us. . . At the stroke of the midnight hour, when the world sleeps, India will awake to life and freedom. . . Freedom and power bring responsibility. . . The achievement we celebrate today is but a step, an opening of opportunity, to the greater triumphs and achievements that await us. Are we brave enough and wise enough to grasp this opportunity and accept the challenge of the future? . . . We have to labour and to work, and work hard, to give reality to our dreams."

Lord Halifax Irwin (ex-Governor General of India) said of Gandhi: "There can be a few men in all history who by personal character and example have been able to so deeply influence the thought of their generation."

On January 30, 1948, as Gandhi entered a prayer meeting, he was shot three times in the chest at close range. Only two days ahead of his death, Gandhi wrote to Rajkumari Amrit Kaur, "If I am to die by the bullet of a mad man, I must do so smiling. There must be no anger within me." Gandhi fulfilled his prophesy. With his final act, he blessed the man who shot him with a smile on his face as he fell to his death. Gandhi's life was ended at age 78, but his example and teachings continue to be a model for others to follow.

"More than 1 million people . . . crowded the funeral route crying, 'Long live Mahatma Gandhi,'"[30] "the world acknowledged his special place when the United Nations flew its flag at half-mast. . . He is the only individual with no connection to any government or international organization for whom this has been done."[31] Albert Einstein wrote, "Generations to come would scarce believe that such a one as this in flesh and blood ever walked on earth."

Conclusion

A monk wrote more than 900 years ago, "When I was a young man, I wanted to change the world. I found it was difficult to change the world, so I tried to change my nation. When I found I couldn't change the nation, I began to focus on my town. I couldn't change the town and as an older man, I tried to change my family. Now, as an old man, I realize the only thing I can change is myself, and suddenly I realize that if long ago I had changed myself, I could have made an impact on my family. My family and I could have made an impact on our town. Their impact could have changed the nation, and I could indeed have changed the world."[32]

ATTRIBUTE 2: CREATOR

*"I do not think there is any thrill that can go through
the human heart like that felt by the inventor."*

– Nikola Tesla

CHAPTER III

CREATION VS. REDISTRIBUTION

"Some regard private enterprise as if it were a predatory
tiger to be shot. Others look upon it as a cow that
they can milk. Only a handful see it for what it really
is—the strong horse that pulls the whole cart."

– Winston Churchill

If you believe in scarcity and a fixed number of resources, you will focus on distributing the limited wealth among society fairly. You will not focus on creation because what currently exists is all there will ever be. Instead of trying to develop a way to divide the current pie, we should focus on creating a new pie big enough for all to share. People who consume more than they create are the only cause of depleting resources and diminishing economics. Fortunately our world is abundant and God has given humans the unique ability to create resources rather than simply use resources. Using our God-given ability to create resources is key to our economic well-being.

The Story of the Farmer and the Thief

Fifteen-year-old Bobby took responsibility for running his family's Arizona farm after his father became ill. Some took unfair advantage of the young man, and crops began disappearing from the fields. Bobby was angry and vowed to catch the thieves and make an example out of them. Vengeance would be his.

As his father was recovering from his illness, Bobby made his rounds through the fields at the end of the day. It was nearly dark. In the distance, he caught sight of someone loading sacks of potatoes into a car. Bobby ran quickly through the field and caught the young thief. His first thought was to take out his frustrations with his fists and then drag the boy to the farmhouse and call the police. He had caught his thief, and he intended to get his just dues.

As Bobby's anger raged, his father pulled up in his pickup. He got out, and placed his weak hand on his son's shoulder and said, "I see you're a bit upset, Bobby. Can I handle this?" He walked over to the young thief and put his arm around his shoulder, looked him in the eye for a moment, and said, "Son, tell me, why are you doing this? Why are you trying to steal these potatoes?"

The young thief replied, "I didn't think you would miss them. You have so very much and I have so very little. Not everyone can be wealthy like you." Then Bobby's father asked the young thief, "Why do you think I have this large farm and comfortable home?" "Because your dad gave them to you," replied the boy. Bobby's father chuckled and put his arm around the young boy. He walked the thief to an area where he could see the undeveloped desert that surrounded the potato farm and said, "Thirty years ago, this is what my potato farm looked like. I originally purchased 10,000 acres of desert land for $27 per acre. Through years of hard work, I transformed the land that was producing very little value into a thriving potato farm which is now worth $3,500 per acre. As a result of years of hard work and industry, I was able to improve this property to the point where now what I purchased for $270,000 is worth $35 million."

The thief's eyes widened and he said in amazement, "Your farm is worth $35 million. Don't you think it is selfish to have so much?" Bobby's father asked, "Selfish, what do you mean?" "Well, if you have so much, that means there is now less for others. Not everyone can be wealthy," stated the young thief.

Bobby's father replied, "When I breathe, does it lessen the amount of oxygen available for you and your family? Is the person who exercises and thus breathes more oxygen selfish because he is taking more than his share of the oxygen?" Perplexed, the young thief replied, "Of course not. There is enough oxygen for everyone to breathe as much as they want." Bobby's father asked, "Why is there plenty of oxygen?" "I don't know. Why?" responded the boy.

Bobby's father explained, "Because oxygen can be created. Since oxygen is created in abundance, we don't have to ration it so we don't run out. Wealth can also be created and thus can be as abundant in our lives as oxygen. We can have as much wealth as we are willing to work to create. To say it is impossible for everyone to be wealthy is as irrational as saying not everyone can breathe as much as he or she wants. The earth is designed to create, produce, and increase. For example, from a single apple seed you can grow a tree that will produce hundreds of apples each year. Two chickens can be multiplied to feed thousands of people. Once we understand that wealth can be created, we will believe that there is enough in the world for everyone to succeed and, as a result, one does not have to become successful at the expense of others. The success of one does not limit another's ability to succeed.

"If every person produced to his or her potential, everyone's needs would be satisfied with a great abundance. For example, the earth is capable of producing food for a population of at least 80 billion, eight times the 10 billion expected to inhabit the earth by the year 2050. One study estimates that with improved scientific methods the earth could feed as many as 1,000 billion people.[33] In 1930, there were approximately 30 million farmers in the United States, barely producing enough food to feed a population of approximately 100 million people. Technological breakthroughs in agriculture during the next fifty years made farming so efficient that by 1980 approximately 3 million farmers were producing enough food for a population of more than 300 million. This represents a 3,000 percent increase in productivity per farmer."[34]

The young thief then asked, "If the world is capable of feeding hundreds of billions of people, why are people starving?"

"This is a great question," continued Bobby's father. "Remember that I said if every person produced to his or her potential, everyone's needs would be satisfied with a great abundance. There are two problems. First, not everyone is producing. Second, there are those who seek wealth by taking what others have produced rather than creating it themselves. When someone seeks wealth by taking someone else's production, they are stealing. Were you creating or stealing when you attempted to take the potatoes from my farm?"

"I was stealing," replied the young thief. Bobby's father continued, "There are some who use the capitalist system to become takers instead of creators. These people are thieves."

Then the young thief asked, "So are businesses and wealth bad things?" In response, Bobby's father continued, "Business and wealth can be good or bad. The question to ask is, 'Was value created or stolen?' Wealth obtained through theft and taking from others depletes resources while wealth obtained by creation and production creates resources and abundance."

The young thief then said, "I have one last question. Why do people believe they can only succeed at the expense of someone else?"

Bobby's father answered, "The root cause is a belief in scarcity, that there is a fixed amount of wealth. With a scarcity belief, if one person gains more financially it means another has less. A great example of scarcity mentality is population control. Those who believe in population control believe there is a fixed pie of resources. Thus, if there are more people, each person will get a smaller piece of the pie. With a scarcity mentality, the only way to increase the quality of life of each individual is to reduce the number of people. Thus as population is reduced, each person receives a larger piece of the pie.

"Good people will not achieve wealth by taking it from others; thus, if they believe the world has a fixed amount of wealth, they will feel guilty the more they receive because that means less for someone else. Once people understand that they can create wealth, they will also understand that as they create wealth they are improving the lives of society—not taking from them. A belief that the world is abundant and that wealth can be created is essential to creating prosperity for you and for society. 'The more we develop an abundance mentality, the more we love to share power and profit and recognition, and the more we are genuinely happy for the successes, well-being, achievements, recognition, and good fortune of other people. We believe that their success adds to—rather than detracts from—our lives.'[35]"

In gratitude, the young thief said, "Thank you for the kindness you have showed me. I have learned a lot today."

Bobby's father invited the young boy to walk with him to the farmhouse. When they got there, Bobby's father asked the young thief what items he and his family needed. He graciously gave them to the boy. Voluntarily, month-by-month, the young would-be thief paid for all the food Bobby's father had given him, including the sacks of potatoes.[36]

Creating a Larger Pie

> *"The more you share profits with your associates—*
> *whether it's in salaries or incentives or bonuses or stock*
> *discounts—the more profit will accrue to the company."*
>
> – Sam Walton, founder of Wal-Mart

It would seem logical that the larger share of ownership you have in a company, the more you will make. This is not always the case, as discovered Hyrum Smith, founder of the Franklin Planner. In 1984, early in the creation of the Franklin Quest Company, Hyrum met with the four men who helped start the company. The purpose of the meeting was to decide ownership interest. As the principal founder, Hyrum could have taken a majority interest in the company. Instead he took only 33 percent and gave 67 percent to the other partners. As the company grew, Hyrum gave away additional portions of his stock to employees. On June 3, 1992, the Franklin Quest Company went public, and its stock began trading on the New York Stock Exchange. The stock Hyrum had given away was now worth more than $200 million while the stock Hyrum retained was only worth $60 million. One of the investment bankers was amazed that Hyrum had given away $200 million. In response, Hyrum said to this investment banker, "If I hadn't given away that stock . . . then the ownership I retained would not have been anywhere near $60 million. . . What I am worth today, I am worth because I was willing to share the wealth."[37]

The investment banker saw that the Franklin Quest stock was worth $260 million in 1992, and Hyrum only had 23 percent of the stock—worth $60 million. The investment banker saw that if Hyrum had retained 50 percent of the company, he would now be worth $130 million instead of $60 million. Hyrum did not believe this was the case. Hyrum believed in abundance and the power of the creation of wealth. Hyrum would rather have a smaller piece of a large pie than a large piece of a small pie. Hypothetically, let's say Hyrum retained the majority interest in the company, 60 percent, and as a result in 1992 the company was smaller and thus only worth $50 million. Hyrum's 60 percent ownership interest would have been worth $30 million or half of what his 23 percent interest in the $260 million company was worth. Would you rather have 60 percent of $50 million ($30 million) or 23 percent of $260 million ($60 million)?

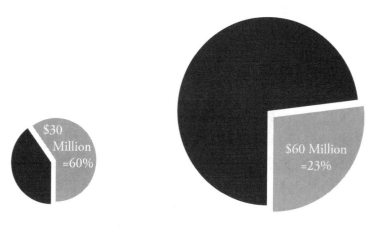

$50 MILLION COMPANY $260 MILLION COMPANY

A similar account is found in the early days of McDonald's. The founder, Ray Kroc, was upset about having to give up 22 percent ownership to fund the operations and growth of the company. One of McDonald's executives said to Mr. Kroc, "You've got to remember, Ray, that 78 percent of something is a lot better than 100 percent of nothing."[38]

United States Case Study on Wealth Creation

The history of America shows how wealth has been created and increased over time (see chart). All dollar amounts in this case study have been adjusted for inflation to their 2005 equivalent values. In 1960, there were 53 million households in the United States with an average income of $50,062 for a total income of $2.65 trillion. In 2000, there were 105 million households in the United States with average income of $88,745 for a total income of $9.37 trillion. Thus, from 1960 to 2000, the population doubled while total income increased 3.5 times. If no new income was created and the population had doubled, income would have been cut in half over the 40 years to $25,000. However, this was not the case, because new wealth was created. The population doubled, and the average income went up by 77 percent.

UNITED STATES CASE STUDY ON WEALTH CREATION				
	1960	1980	2000	Increase
Total U.S. Personal Income[39]	$2.65 trillion	$5.26 trillion	$9.37 trillion	3.5 Times
Total U.S. Households[40]	53 million	80 million	105 million	2.0 Times
Average Household Income	$50,062	$65,414	$88,745	77%
All Dollar Amounts in 2005 Equivalents				

Through work and industry, Americans increased their income from $2.65 trillion to more than $9 trillion. Our focus should be working to create rather than redistributing the current wealth.

Benjamin Franklin: Inspiring Creator

"As we enjoy great advantages from the inventions of others, we should be glad of an opportunity to serve others by any invention of ours; and this we should do freely and generously."

– Benjamin Franklin

"The rise of Benjamin Franklin (1706-1790) from modest beginnings to a station among the most accomplished Americans of his day has long been recognized as one of the world's great success stories."[41] Throughout his life he was a creator, making many important contributions to society as an author, businessman, inventor, philanthropist, and civil servant.

Author

Franklin was a very prolific reader and writer. In his autobiography he wrote, "From my infancy I was passionately fond of reading, and all the money that came into my hands was laid out in the purchasing of books."[42] One of Franklin's most successful creations was the *Poor Richard's Almanac* which he began publishing at the end of 1732. *Poor Richard's Almanac* "combined the two goals of his doing-well-by-doing-good philosophy: the making of money and the promotion of virtue. It became, in the course of its twenty-five-year run, America's great humor classic."[43] Franklin wrote of the *Almanac*, "I endeavored to make it both entertaining and useful, and it accordingly came to be in such demand, that I reaped considerable profit from it, vending annually near ten thousand. And observing that it was generally read . . . I considered it as a proper vehicle for conveying instruction. . . I therefore filled all the little spaces that occurred . . . with proverbial sentences [on] industry and frugality . . . as the means of procuring wealth, and . . . securing virtue."[44] Here are a few of the proverbs from the Almanac:

"Keep your eyes wide open before marriage, half shut afterwards."

"An ounce of prevention is worth a pound of cure."

"Search others for their virtues, thyself for thy vices."

"Dost thou love life? Then do not squander time, for that's the stuff life is made of."

"He that lies down with dogs shall rise up with fleas."

"A good example is the best sermon."

"Beware of little expenses; a small leak will sink a great ship."

"Love your enemies, for they will tell you your faults."

"In his final edition [of the almanac], Franklin would sum things up with a fictional speech by an old man named Father Abraham who strings together all of Poor Richard's adages about the need for frugality and virtue. . . [The speech] was published as *The Way to Wealth* and became, for a time, the most famous book to come out of colonial America."[45]

Businessman

In 1728 at age 22, Franklin opened a printing shop in Philadelphia. Franklin wrote in his autobiography, "We had scarce . . . put our press in order, before George House, an acquaintance of mine, brought a countryman to us, who he had met in the street inquiring for a printer. . . This countryman's five shillings, being our first-fruits, and coming so seasonably, gave me more pleasure than any crown I have since earned."[46]

The opinion in the town was that Franklin's print shop would fail as there were already two printers in the place. Franklin's industry and dedication made the business a success. Franklin worked hard to do a great job for his customers to win referral business and also developed a profitable newspaper and the *Poor Richard's Almanac*. Dr. Baird, one of the town's prominent merchants, wrote, "For the industry of that Franklin is superior to anything I ever saw of the kind; I see him still at work when I go home from club, and he is at work again before his neighbors are out of bed."[47]

"By the early 1730s, Franklin's business was thriving. He started building an extended little empire by sending his young workers, once they had served their time with him, to set up partnership shops in places ranging from Charleston to Hartford. He would supply the presses and part of the expenses, as well as some content for the publications, and in return take a portion of the revenue."[48]

Franklin was grateful to Dr. Baird and others who helped him when starting his business and worked throughout his life to help other young beginners. As part of his will, Franklin gave 1,000 pounds (approximately $4,400) to the city of Boston and another 1,000 pounds to the city of Philadelphia. To prevent the cities from spending the money, Franklin required that the money be placed in a trust fund and then invested and used to provide loans to "married tradesman under the age of 26" to get them started in business. During the two hundred years of the trust, money was loaned to hundreds of individuals. The trust fund in Philadelphia grew to $2.25 million, and the trust fund in Boston grew to $5 million.[49] Benjamin Franklin understood the power of compounding interest. He wrote, "Remember that money is of a prolific generating nature. Money can beget money, and its offspring can beget more, and so on. Five shillings turned is six, turned again it is seven and threepence, and so on, till it becomes an hundred pounds."[50]

"His devotion to key financial principles allowed him to retire at the young age of 42. It was at this point that he began to convert his money back into time in the form of an early retirement. During the next 42 years, before his death at age 84, he accomplished the unbelievable. Most of us do not have this extra time for such accomplishments—not because we don't manage our time well, but rather because we spend most of our life converting time into money."[51]

Benjamin Franklin gave this advice to a young tradesman in 1748: "The way to wealth, if you desire it, is as plain as the way to market. It depends chiefly on two words, industry and frugality; that is waste neither time nor money, but make the best use of both . . . I will acquaint you with the true secret of money-catching, the certain way to fill empty purses, and how to keep them always full. Two simple rules, well observed, will do the business. First, let honesty and industry be thy constant companions; and secondly, spend less than you earn . . . then shalt thou reach the point of happiness, and independence."[52]

Inventor

Franklin was one of America's most prominent inventors, having created an Armonica, the Pennsylvania fireplace, America's first catheter, fertilizer, the lightning rod, bifocals, and the odometer.

Pennsylvania Fireplace

In the early 1740s, Franklin invented "a wood-burning stove that could be built into fireplaces to maximize heat while minimizing smoke and drafts. Using his knowledge of convection and heat transfer, Franklin came up with an ingenious design."[53] In 1744, Franklin began manufacturing and marketing the stove throughout the northeast.

Fertilizer

Franklin discovered that gypsum, a rock similar to limestone, could be pulverized into a powder called land plaster and applied to the field as a fertilizer. Franklin told his neighbors that using gypsum land plaster as a fertilizer would increase their crop yields. They did not believe him and argued that gypsum land plaster was of no use to crops. To prove his point, "Franklin [sowed] land plaster in a clover field near one of the main roads in Pennsylvania as to form the sentence, 'This has been plastered with gypsum,' and the letters were detected readily by the height and color of the clover where the gypsum had been sown."[54]

Since Franklin's discovery, several studies have compared fields using gypsum land plaster to fields that have not. The studies found that "one bushel of gypsum spread over an acre of land fit for its action may add more than 20 times its own weight to a single crop of clover hay."[55] Franklin had created a way to dramatically increase crop yields.

Lightning Rod

In the summer of 1743 while visiting Boston, Franklin came across a traveling scientific showman from Scotland who performed tricks with electricity. Franklin wrote of the experiments, "Being on a subject quite new to me, they equally surprised and pleased me. . . I eagerly seized the opportunity of repeating what I had seen at Boston; and by much practice, acquired great readiness in performing those [and] adding a number of new ones."[56]

Franklin was engrossed with the study of electricity, performing many experiments, with some of them knocking him down with painful shocks. He discovered many important properties of electricity but had yet to find practical applications. He wrote, "[I am] chagrined a little that we have been hitherto able to produce nothing in this way of use to mankind."[57] He then joked that the shock could be used to humble people saying, "If there is no other use discovered of electricity this however is something considerable, that it may help to make a vain man humble."[58]

"In the journal he kept for his experiments, Franklin noted in November 1749 some intriguing similarities between electrical sparks and lightning. . . For centuries, the devastating scourge of lightning had generally been considered a supernatural phenomenon or expression of God's will. At the approach of a storm, church bells were rung to ward off the bolts. 'The tones of the consecrated metal repel the demon and avert storm and lightning,' declared St. Thomas Aquinas. But even the most religiously faithful were likely to have noticed this was not very effective. During one thirty-five-year period in Germany alone during the mid-1700s, 386 churches were struck and more than one hundred bell ringers killed."[59] Franklin later wrote to Harvard professor John Winthrop saying, "The lightning seems to strike steeples of choice and at the very time the bells are ringing; yet still they continue to bless the new bells and jangle the old one whenever it thunders. One would think it was now time to try some other trick."[60]

Franklin believed if his assumption that lightning was electricity was correct, than lightning rods could be used to protect homes, ships, churches, and other structures from one of the greatest natural dangers people face. This led to his most famous experiment to collect charges from lightning into a Leyden jar to test against electricity produced in his lab. Franklin developed a silk kite with a sharp wire extended from the top of the kite to attempt to collect charges from lightning. He then attached a key to the base of the string so that sparks could be drawn from the key by a wire. In June 1752 as a storm gathered, Franklin and his son, William, flew the kite. After a while the string on the kite tightened and Franklin put his knuckle near the key and drew a spark. Franklin then proceeded to collect charges into a Leyden jar and discovered that lightning had the same properties as electricity. That summer Franklin had two grounded lightning rods erected on two high buildings in Philadelphia and also placed one on his home.

"Lightning rods began sprouting across Europe and the colonies. Franklin was suddenly a famous man. Harvard and Yale gave him honorary degrees in the summer of 1753. . . Few scientific discoveries have been of such immediate service to humanity. . . In solving of the universe's greatest mysteries, he had conquered one of nature's most terrifying dangers."[61]

Philanthropist

Junto Club

In the fall of 1727, Franklin created a club to work on improving themselves, their businesses, and the community. He wrote, "I had formed most of my ingenious acquaintance into a club of mutual improvement, which was called the Junto; we met on Friday evenings."[62] The members of the Junto Club assisted in many of Franklin's projects and creations.

The Library Company of Philadelphia

In 1731, Franklin, with the help of the other Junto members, created America's first circulating library so that people would have access to a greater number of books. Also, people would be able to borrow books even though they might not be able to afford to buy them. Franklin wrote, "These libraries have improved the general conversation of the Americans, made the common tradesmen and farmers as intelligent as most gentlemen from other countries, and perhaps have contributed in some degree to the stand so generally made throughout the colonies in defense of their privileges."[63] The Library Company of Philadelphia, which had 375 titles in 1741, has now grown to over 500,000 books with thousands visiting the library each year.

University of Pennsylvania

Franklin was a strong proponent of education and wanted to establish a college in Pennsylvania. "In 1749, Benjamin Franklin presented his vision for a new type of learning institution, that unlike other American Colonial colleges, would not focus on education for the clergy, but would instead prepare students for lives of business and public service. The proposed program of study would become the nation's first modern liberal arts curriculum."[64] Franklin wrote in the pamphlet entitled *Proposals Relating to the Education of Youth in Pennsylvania*, "The good education of youth has been esteemed by wise men in all ages, as the surest foundation of the happiness both of private families and of commonwealths. . . [Education should cultivate] an inclination, joined with an ability, to serve mankind, one's country, friends, and family . . . and should, indeed, be the great aim and end of all learning."[65]

Franklin raised the funds for the academy and created a detailed proposal of the topics to be taught with "exhaustive procedures on the best ways to teach everything from pronunciation to military history."[66] The academy opened in January of 1751 (known as the University of Pennsylvania by 1791) with Franklin serving as the president of the board. The University of Pennsylvania continues to thrive with a current enrollment of over 24,000 students and hundreds of thousands of alumni.

Pennsylvania Hospital

Franklin founded America's first hospital in Philadelphia with the help of Dr. Thomas Bond. The idea for the hospital was Dr. Bond's, and he approached Franklin to assist in its creation. In 1751, Franklin published articles in the *Pennsylvania Gazette* to create interest in and donation to the construction of the hospital. In August 1751 he wrote, "The good particular men may do separately in relieving the sick, is small, compared with what they may do collectively; or by a joint endeavour and interest. Hence the erecting of hospitals . . . for the reception, entertainment, and cure of the sick poor, has been found by experience exceedingly beneficial, as they turn out annually great numbers of patients perfectly cured, who might otherwise have been lost to their families, and to society."[67]

"With Franklin's talent for popularizing an idea, funds were obtained from both the Pennsylvania legislature and private citizens in 1751; Franklin received a promise from the legislature to match whatever he collected from the public. This fundraising method, now known as a matching fund drive, was a new technique. Another fundraising idea of Franklin's was the sale of a promotional booklet, Some Account of the Pennsylvania Hospital (1756); this served as an early 'development report' and came complete with a contribution form on the last page!"[68] With some creative fundraising, Franklin acquired the needed funds and wrote, "A convenient and handsome building was soon erected; the institution has by constant experience been found useful, and flourishes."[69] The hospital continues to serve the public more than 250 years later, with "over 29,000 inpatient admissions and 115,000 outpatient visits each year, including over 5,200 births."[70]

Civil Servant

"Of all the founding fathers, Franklin has the unique distinction of having signed all three of the major documents that freed the colonies from British rule and established the United States as an independent nation: the Declaration of Independence, The Treaty of Paris, and the United States Constitution."[71]

The signing of the Declaration of Independence was a solemn act, and required great firmness and patriotism. It was treason against the government of Great Britain—an offense that was punishable by death. At the signing, Franklin is quoted as having replied to a comment by John Hancock that they must all hang together saying, "Yes, we must, indeed, all hang together, or most assuredly we shall all hang separately,"[72] This play on words suggested that if they failed to stay united and win the revolution, they would surely each be tried and executed, individually, for treason.

During the Revolutionary War, Franklin served as the Minister to France from 1778 to 1785. Franklin "successfully negotiated a treaty of alliance between the French and the united colonies and had secured loans from the French government which helped finance the American Revolution against the British."[73] The Revolutionary War officially ended thanks in part to Franklin's diplomacy during the negotiations on the Treaty of Paris, which resulted in the world's greatest superpowers, France and Great Britain, recognizing the United States as "free sovereign and independent states."[74]

Following the victory in the Revolutionary War, the American colonies had the unique opportunity of establishing a new country and government. The Articles of Confederation were the first governing document that loosely tied the newly independent thirteen colonies, but they were incomplete and inadequate to completely govern the new nation. To establish a constitution and a new form of government, the Constitutional Convention was organized and held in Philadelphia from May 25 to September 17, 1787. George Washington presided over the convention, and with 54 other great leaders, one of whom was Benjamin Franklin, they drafted the Constitution.

In September 1787 the Constitution was completed and ready to be signed; however, many of the 55 delegates were unhappy. Franklin delivered a passionate speech "in which he used his persuasive powers to urge all delegates to sign the Constitution."[75] He said in part, "I confess that I do not entirely approve of this Constitution at present . . . For when you assemble a number of men to have the advantage of their joint wisdom, you inevitably assemble with those men all their prejudices, their passions, their errors of opinion, their local interests, and their selfish views. From such an assembly can a perfect production be expected? It therefore astonishes me, Sir, to find this system approaching so near to perfection as it does; and I think it will astonish our enemies. . . I hope therefore that for our own sakes, as a part of the people, and for the sake of our posterity, we shall act heartily and unanimously in recommending this Constitution."[76] Following Franklin's speech, the Constitution was signed. "Whilst the last members were signing, Dr. Franklin, looking towards the president's chair, at the back of which a rising sun happened to be painted, observed to a few members near him, that painters had often found it difficult, in their art, to distinguish a rising from a setting sun. I have, said he, often and often, in the course of the session, and the vicissitude of my hopes and fears as to its issue, looked at that behind the president, without being able to tell whether it was rising or setting; but now, at length, I have the happiness to know that it is a rising and not a setting sun."[77] It was a rising sun indeed. The United States of America now has over 300 million citizens, with a combined annual income of more than $9 trillion.

Legacy of Creation

Franklin died on April 17, 1790, at age 84. "It is estimated that 20,000 mourners gathered for the funeral. When Franklin had arrived in Philadelphia's port on October 6, 1723, he was a broke runaway. Now the ships in the very same harbor Franklin had arrived in flew their flags at half-mast for the man who had enriched the world."[78] Franklin spent his life creating, and over 250 years later his work continues to bless the lives of millions. What will be your legacy of creation?

Conclusion

Abraham Lincoln taught, "It is best for all to leave each man free to acquire property as fast as he can. Some will get wealthy. I don't believe in a law to prevent a man from getting rich; it would do more harm than good. . . When one starts poor, as most do in the race of life, free society is such that he knows he can better his condition. . . I am not ashamed to confess that twenty-five years ago I was a hired laborer. . . I want every man to have the chance . . . in which he can better his condition—when he may look forward and hope to be a hired laborer this year and the next, work for himself afterward, and finally to hire men to work for him. That is the true system. . . Property is the fruit of labor; property is desirable; is a positive good in the world. That some should be rich, shows that others may become rich, and hence is just encouragement to industry and enterprise. Let not him who is houseless pull down the house of another; but let him labor diligently and build one for himself."[79]

Attribute 3: Independent

"Every handout has a price and that price is a loss of freedom. We must preserve our talents of self-sufficiency, our ability to create things for ourselves, and our true love of independence."

– Cameron C. Taylor

Chapter IV

Avoid Harmful Help

*"Charity is injurious unless it helps the
recipient to become independent of it."*
– John D. Rockefeller, Jr.

There's a story about a wealthy family in which the father had
built a large and very successful business from the ground up. As
the father approached retirement, he called his son into his office
and told his son that he wanted him to eventually take over his
company. The son was excited and asked, "When are you going
to give it to me?" The father replied, "I am not going to give
you anything, you must earn it." The son replied, "How am I
supposed to do that?"

The father answered, "First, you must earn $10,000 to
purchase a small portion of ownership in the company." As the
son left to begin his quest, his mother grabbed him and shoved
$10,000 into his hand and told him to give the money to his
father. Thrilled by his good fortune, the son ran to his father.
His dad was sitting by the fireplace reading a book. The son
approached his father and said, "Dad, Dad, here's $10,000 for
the business." Without looking up, the father took the money
and tossed it into the fire. The son stood, frozen with amazement
and watched. As the money burned, the father said, "Come back
when you have earned the money."

As he left the room, his mother once again gave him $10,000

and told him to be more convincing in selling his father on the idea that he had actually worked for the money. So the boy scuffed himself up a little, jogged around the block a few times, and then went to find his father again. His father was still sitting in front of the fireplace reading a book. The boy approached his father and said, "It sure is tough earning money. Here's the $10,000. I really do want to own the business." Once again the father took the $10,000 and tossed it in the fireplace. As the money burned, the son asked, "How did you know I didn't earn the money?" The father replied, "It is easy to lose or spend money that is not your own."

At this point, the son realized he wasn't going to get the business unless he actually earned the $10,000. He wanted the business, so when his mother offered him the money again, he declined her offer. He went out and picked up some odd jobs.

His jobs required him to get up early and stay up late, but he worked and worked until he earned $10,000. Proudly, he walked into his father's office and presented him with the money. Like before, his father was sitting by the fire reading a book. And like before, the father took the money and threw it in the fireplace. As the money hit the flames, the son dove to the floor, and stuck his hands into the fire and pulled out the money. The father looked his son in the eyes and said, "I see you really did earn the money this time."

Harmful Help as a Parent

A business owner and church leader shared this experience: "I remember some years ago, a young man and his wife and little children moved to our Arizona community. As we got acquainted with them, he told me of the rigorous youth he had spent as he grew up. He'd had to get up at five and six o'clock in the morning and go out and deliver papers. He'd had to work on the farm and he'd had to do many things that were still rankling [irritation/ resentment] in his soul. Then he concluded with this statement: 'My boys are never going to have to do that.' And we saw his boys grow up and you couldn't get them to do anything."

Many parents make the mistake of providing damaging financial assistance to their children. With good intentions, they want to help their children get started in life and offer assistance when a financial need arises. Unfortunately, the result is often opposite to the one desired. Instead of helping children become self-sufficient, the children become dependent. Rather than sparking initiative and discipline, they become idle and indulgent. Instead of being achievement oriented, they become entitlement oriented. Instead of becoming grateful, they become demanding. "Children who always get what they want will want as long as they live."[80] Research has shown that "in general, the more dollars adult children receive [from their parents] the fewer they accumulate, while those who are given fewer dollars accumulate more."[81]

How can we make sure our children grow up with the earning mentality rather than the entitlement mentality? One of the best ways to create an earning mentality in our children is to teach them how to work. However, there is a growing trend of fewer and fewer children working. As parents are providing financially for all their children's needs, many children are no longer working during the summer. In 2007, for the first time on record the majority of U.S. teenagers were not working or looking for work at the beginning of the summer. Only 49% of teens age 16 to 19 were working or looking for work in June 2007, a steep decline from the 68% of teens working or looking for work in June 1978.[82]

There is another trend that I believe is tied to the trend of fewer teens working at jobs. As the number of teens working has gone down, the number of adult children returning to live with their parents has increased. Census figures indicate that more than 80 million so-called "empty nesters" now find themselves with at least one grown child living at home.[83] The common parental expectation of having an "empty nest" has given way to the reality of a "crowded nest." And a recent survey revealed that 25% of the college graduating class expected to live at home after graduating.[84]

To help teach children good work ethics, parents need to look for opportunities for their children to work. I have a 6-year-old son and he never asks me for money. When there is something he wants, he asks me for jobs he can do to earn the money to purchase the item. He has learned that Mom and Dad will not give him money, but that money has to be earned. I have him help when I do various mailers for my companies. When I come home with the mailers, my son is so excited that he will often yell something along the lines of, "Yes! Dad brought home mailers." It is fun to see a 6-year-old so excited about working and earning money.

Parents should also create a financial environment that requires their children to work and earn money by having a job outside of the home to pay for their expenses in their youth and pay their own way through college. I've found that those who had jobs outside of the home while in high school and college have a stronger work ethic than those who did not. Having noticed this trend leads me to believe that teaching a child to work is not simply teaching them how to complete tasks or earn money, but it is teaching a way of life. Now as I hire employees, I seek to find those who have strong work ethic by asking what jobs they had during high school and college. The hardest working employees I have had are those who had to work their way through high school and college.

If you keep your children from experiencing struggle and responsibility, you will also prevent them from growing. Work ethic, discipline, and initiative cannot be purchased with money, but instead are developed through work, experience, and education. Living off others is a form of bondage—for if you take from a person his responsibility to care for himself, you also take from him the opportunity to be free. If you help too much, you will make an individual helpless. Do not give your kids money; give them education and opportunity. It costs a lot less and will develop the productive, self-sufficient children you desire.

The Story of the Caterpillar

While starting my first business, I often relied on one of my business partners and mentors who was a multimillionaire for advice. My business was growing, but it struggled to turn a profit. I continued to work hard, but things were getting tighter and tighter financially. I went to my rich partner and asked for a small monthly salary or a loan to help me get by until the business was profitable. He declined to give me any assistance. I was frustrated and said, "You are making millions a year, and I am struggling to stay alive. Please help me." He looked at me and I could tell he was close to giving in and wanted to help me. "However," he replied, "If I take away your struggle, I will also take away your victory." He then shared the following story:

"There was a young boy who came across a caterpillar hanging in a cocoon. He visited the cocoon several times a day, watching it grow and change and waiting for a butterfly to emerge. After a few days, the young boy began to see the cocoon move and watched as a butterfly struggled to emerge. The boy wanted to help the caterpillar so he ran home and got a pair of scissors. He returned and carefully cut open the cocoon and out fell a partially developed butterfly. This caterpillar would never fly as a butterfly. The young boy had innocently killed the butterfly he was trying to help." At the time, I didn't find this advice helpful, but today I am grateful to a wise partner and mentor who resisted the temptation to cut open my cocoon.

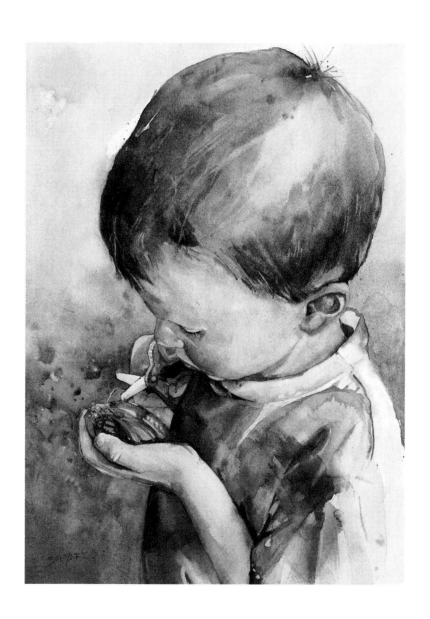

CHAPTER V

TAKE THE INITIATIVE

"Everything you want is just outside your comfort zone."
– Robert Allen

"The world bestows its big prizes, both in money and honors, for but one thing. And that is initiative. What is initiative? I'll tell you: It is doing the right thing without being told. But next to doing the thing without being told is to do it when you are told once . . . but their pay is not always in proportion. Next, there are those who never do a thing until they are told twice: such get no honors and small pay. Next, there are those who do the right thing only when necessity kicks them from behind, and these get indifference instead of honors, and a pittance for pay. . . Then, still lower down in the scale than this, we have the fellow who will not do the right thing even when someone goes along to show him how and stays to see that he does it: he is always out of a job. . . To which class do you belong?"[85]

The Wright Brothers

The lives of the Wright brothers provide many wonderful examples of taking the initiative. William J. Tate, a man who helped the Wright brothers in assembling the Wrights' first glider in North Carolina, wrote of the early flights, "The mental attitude of the natives toward the Wrights was that they were a simple pair of harmless cranks that were wasting their time at a fool attempt to do something that was impossible. The chief argument against their success could be heard at the stores and post office, and ran something like this: 'God didn't intend man to fly. If He did, He would have given him a set of wings on his shoulders.'"[86]

Wilber was born in 1867 and Orville was born in 1871 to Susan and Milton Wright in the Midwest. Orville and Wilber's interest in flying began in 1878 when their father gave them a toy helicopter.[87] This interest turned into an active pursuit at the end of the 19th century. Wilber began reading "everything he could lay his hands on, everything in sight. His father had some simple books on flight in nature in his library, and the Dayton Public Library had a handful of things on flight. When he had exhausted the local resources, Wilbur wrote to the Smithsonian Institution asking for more information on flight."[88]

In 1899, they began their flight experiments. At this time, the Wright brothers were running a bicycle repair and sales shop. The revenues from this company supported their living expenses and funded the development of the airplane. During the next four years, the Wright brothers performed thousands of tests, experiments, and flights. In 1901, they created the world's first wind tunnel and tested more than 200 different wing shapes,[89] and just in the months of September and October of 1902 they made over 700 glides.[90] On December 17, 1903, Orville, age 32, and Wilber, age 36, achieved their dream of a controlled, powered flight. The flight covered a distance of 120 feet in 12 seconds—about half the length of a 747 jumbo jet. This flight was the beginning of modern aviation.

In 1904, the Wright brothers decided to take a financial risk and withdraw from the bicycle business to focus on developing a practical airplane they could sell. Wilbur explained to an acquaintance, "We believed that if we would take the risk of devoting our entire time and financial resources we could conquer the difficulties in the path to success . . . as our financial future was at stake [we] were compelled to regard it as a strict business proposition."[91] They would have to make the airplane a profitable business to survive, but they never compromised their values. The Wright brothers expected their employees to observe their family rules, and among those who worked for them "there was no drinking, gambling, or flying on Sundays."[92]

In February 1908, the company obtained a contract from the U.S. Army to build a two-seat aircraft that could fly for an hour at an average speed of 40 miles per hour and land undamaged. In July 1909, they completed a flight that met the U.S. Army's requirements and received $30,000 ($645,000 in 2006 dollars) for their aircraft. In 1910, they added air shows and commercial air cargo shipping to their business, earning nearly $100,000 ($2 million in 2006 dollars) in profit that year.[93]

Flying was a risky venture. Otto Lilienthal, an early aviator pioneer whose work assisted and inspired the Wright brothers, died after a gust of wind threw his glider out of balance, causing him to fall fifty feet and break his spine. His last words were quoted as "sacrifices must be made," and those words were carved on his tombstone.[94] The brothers wrote of Lilienthal and other early aviator pioneers that their work "infected us with their own unquenchable enthusiasm, and transformed idle curiosity into the active zeal of workers."[95]

Orville and Wilber experienced their share of crashes. One occurred on September 17, 1908, when a propeller malfunctioned and the aircraft crashed, killing the passenger. Orville suffered multiple serious injuries, including a broken leg and broken ribs. Because of the dangers in flying, and at the request of their father,

Wilber and Orville never flew together. However, on May 25, 1910, after they had made many improvements that increased the safety of the airplane, and for the sake of history, the father agreed to let Wilber and Orville fly together. This was the only time the brothers flew together. After this flight, Orville took his 81-year-old father on the only flight of his life, which lasted 6 minutes and 55 seconds. "At one point during the flight, Milton leaned close to his son's ear and shouted . . . 'Higher, Orville, higher!'"[96]

Wilber died from typhoid fever in 1912 at age 45. "Twenty-five thousand people viewed his casket and for three full minutes the citizens of Dayton stopped everything they were doing as they mourned an American hero. Orville had lost his brother, his best friend, his other half who knew the secrets of flying. He was devastated, but he carried on."[97] Orville continued to run the

Wright Company for three more years until he was 44 years old. On October 15, 1915, Orville sold his interest in the company. "*The New York Times* reported that Orville received roughly $1.5 million [$30 million in 2006 dollars], plus an additional $25,000 [$500,000 in 2006 dollars] for his services as chief consulting engineer during the first year of the new company's operation."[98] God did not give men wings upon their shoulders, but He did give them minds and hands to create. It took faith, study, courage, work, and persistence to achieve the miracle of flight. Two men with a dream to fly created wings for us all—the wings God intended for man.

The Wright brothers should inspire each of us to ask, "What cause or endeavor can I take the initiative to move forward?"

ATTRIBUTE 4: HUMBLE

"When a man is wrapped up in himself,
he makes a pretty small package."

– John Ruskin

CHAPTER VI

CONTINUALLY SEEK IMPROVEMENT

*"True nobility is in being superior
to your own previous self."*
– Hindu Proverb

Life is like trying to go up a downward escalator in that if you're not stepping up (putting forth effort), you're going down. Life is not like a stairway upon which you can reach a certain step and then stop and maintain your position. Just as a tree is either growing or decaying, so we are either progressing or regressing. In life, you cannot be at a standstill.

Don Soderquist, retired senior vice chairman of the board for Wal-Mart, shares this story: "I was at a banquet one evening and had the opportunity to visit with Harry Cunningham, the former CEO of K-Mart stores. In fact, he was the legendary character who dramatically changed retail in America by developing the concept of the K-Mart stores for the former Kresge company—a model we carefully studied and considered when developing Wal-Mart stores. I thanked him for what he had done in pioneering the successful discounting format as we know it today. He was gracious in accepting my praise, but was quick to add how much he appreciated what Wal-Mart had done in developing the concept even further. He went on to say, 'We made a serious mistake along the way by not changing and updating our stores over the years. We had a successful formula that was working and saw no reason to change. You folks at Wal-Mart continued to improve until you were much better than we were, and by that time, you passed us by.' The lesson for me in that conversation was that while success can lead to success, it could also lead to failure if you refuse to focus on improving."[99]

Growth and the 80/20 Rule

It is by pushing ourselves to our current maximum that we open the door of growth to a new maximum. For example, much of the growth from weightlifting comes from the final reps before you can lift no more. If you could bench press 200 pounds a maximum of 10 reps, 80 percent of muscle growth and increased strength will result from the final two reps and 20 percent of the growth results from the first eight reps. The last two reps are the hardest, but if neglected will cost you 80 percent of your growth. It does not require twice the effort to achieve twice the improvement, because the final efforts of maximum exertion result in exponential returns.

In business, if you were to simply work an additional 40 minutes a day, which could be achieved by taking your lunch to work and eating quickly in your office instead of going out to lunch, you would complete an additional month of fulltime work each year. While 40 minutes a day represents only an 8 percent increase in hours worked (based on an 8-hour workday), it could translate into twice the pay.

Conclusion

The great football coach Vince Lombardi taught: "Constantly seek ways to do better whatever needs to be done. If a person with this quality will continue positive application of this negative factor, that person will have a leadership role. The quality: dissatisfaction. To make the unsatisfactory satisfactory or better is the mark of leadership. Never be satisfied with less than top performance, and progress will be the reward." Each time we achieve a goal we should ask, How can it be done better? How can it be improved? "Never [be] satisfied with the status quo or with past attainments. Reaching a goal is merely a signal to set a higher one; goal-setting is done in small increments so that people never become discouraged: at the same time, they are never permanently satisfied."[100]

Captain James Cook, an 18th-century English explorer, showed the spirit of excellence by saying of his many voyages of discovery, "I had an ambition, not only to go farther than any man had ever been before, but I wanted to go as far as it was possible for any man to go." Life should be a never-ending quest for improvement.

CHAPTER VII

BE TEACHABLE

"Listen to advice and accept instruction,
and in the end you will be wise."
– Proverbs 19:20

The weakest part of each person is where he or she thinks himself or herself the wisest. In the words of the great basketball coach John Wooden, "It's what we learn after we think we know it all that really counts." Those who are teachable and continually seek to improve and grow rarely contract the disease of pride.

Benjamin Franklin taught, "An investment in knowledge always pays the best interest."[101] Education and transportation are tools that get us to our destination. Over the years transportation has moved from the horse and buggy to trains, cars, and airplanes. Each new mode of transportation has enabled us to reach our destination in a shorter period of time. In the 1800s it took months to cross the plains to the west. Today, with improved tools, we can make the same journey in a matter of hours. Education is also a tool that can speed up your journey to financial independence and prosperity. Studies of those with a high net worth have revealed that they spend significant time each month on financial education.[102] Studies also show there is direct correlation between the amount of time spent on financial education and net worth. The more you learn, the more you earn.

There are three resources I look to for financial education:
1. Reading books
2. Attending seminars
3. Listening to audio programs

Reading Books

"Reading is to the mind what exercise is to the body: as by the one, health is preserved, strengthened, and invigorated; by the other, virtue (which is the health of the mind) is kept alive, cherished, and confirmed."[103] "When we read inspired, thought-provoking books, we grow richer in all phases of our lives. In short, reading has the power to transform us from what we are right now to what we could be in the future."[104]

Reading is a shortcut to success. The Greek philosopher Socrates taught, "Employ your time in improving yourself by other men's writings, so that you shall gain easily what others have labored hard for."[105] A book provides a powerful way to learn in a few hours what others have learned in a lifetime.

Block out time each day to read positive, inspiring books. In 2006, the average American watched 4 hours and 45 minutes of television a day and read 18 minutes a day from books.[106] As you spend more time reading books on positive, inspiring, and financial topics, you will see an increase in your net worth. The libraries of the world are full of knowledge free for the taking but "the man who does not read good books has no advantage over the man who can't read."[107]

Attending Seminars

In addition to reading, you can attend seminars and workshops designed to help you achieve your dreams. Robert Kiyosaki, author of *Rich Dad, Poor Dad,* wrote, "I go to seminars.

I like it when they are at least two days long because I like to immerse myself in a subject. In 1973, I was watching TV and this guy came on advertising a three-day seminar on how to buy real estate for nothing down . . . and that course has made me at least $2 million, if not more. But most importantly, it bought me life. I don't have to work for the rest of my life because of that one course. I go to at least two such courses every year."[108]

Listening to Audio Programs

The national average commute to work is 24 minutes. How do you spend time in your car? Why not utilize driving time learning the principles that will bring success in every facet of your life? There are audio programs and audio books to teach you on every topic imaginable. If you want to increase your net worth, decide to make your time in the car a time for education instead of a time for entertainment.

To get started, check out the audio book selection at your local library and utilize this form of education while commuting, during flights, or even on your iPod while exercising. Many people ask how many songs their iPod holds. I ask how many audio books it can hold.

"The illiterate of the 21st century will not be those who cannot read and write, but those who cannot learn, unlearn, and relearn."[109]

The Cost of Pride

During the French and Indian War, the British General Edward Braddock, age 60 at the time, employed the help of a Virginia militia. When one of the young 23-year-old Virginian soldiers who was well acquainted with the Indian mode of warfare modestly offered his advice, the haughty Braddock said, "What! An American buskin teach a British General how to fight!"[110] Braddock did not heed the advice and the British suffered a disastrous defeat and General Braddock was wounded by a shot through the right arm and into his lung. Following the injury to General Braddock, that same 23-year-old, with no official position in the chain of command, was able to lead and maintain some order and formed a rear guard, which allowed them to evacuate and eventually disengage. This earned him the title of "Hero of the Monongahela." General Braddock was carried off the field by George Washington, the soldier whose advice he had rejected. Braddock died on July 13, 1755, four days after the battle. Before he died, Braddock left Washington the blood-stained sash of his uniform. Washington carried the sash with him for the remainder of his life. Perhaps he carried the sash as a reminder of the cost of pride and of the necessity of being humble and teachable if he was to be successful in his efforts. Had Braddock listened to the advice of young George Washington, his life may have been saved.

George Washington was teachable and spent time each day reading. During his lifetime, Washington accumulated a library of more than 700 books, a great many which he studied closely. Washington's step-granddaughter, Nelly Custis, wrote to one of Washington's early biographers saying, "It was his custom to retire to his library at nine or ten o'clock, where he remained an hour before he went to his chamber. He always arose before the sun, and remained in his library until called to breakfast."

CHAPTER VIII

BE HUMBLE

"Humility is the most difficult of all virtues to achieve;
nothing dies harder than the desire to think well of oneself."
– T. S. Eliot

A person who is humble is teachable, seeks to do their best, is self-reliant, mission driven, and grateful. In the words of the Bengali poet Rabindranath Tagore, "We come nearest to the great when we are great in humility."

A humble person is genuinely interested in what others have to say. They know they do not have all the answers and continually seek to learn from the insights and experiences of others—they "approach others with open minds and are willing to be taught."[111] The humble usually listen more than they talk. Of their accomplishments, the humble will most likely say nothing or something along the lines of "God has done it" or "We have done it." The humble acknowledge the work, help, and support of others and give thanks to them and God. Exercising ego in public is not the way to build an effective organization. One person seeking glory does not accomplish much.

The humble realize that life is not a competition. They are not worried about how they are doing in relation to others but whether or not they are doing their personal best. The humble are cooperative and always seek to lift others. They celebrate the success of others. Humble people consider themselves smart, beautiful, or athletic, but they will not think themselves prettier, smarter, or a better athlete than others. Life is not a competition with others. Life is a competition with yourself—to do your personal best each day.

For the humble, their worth and respect comes from within. Self-reliance is their source of worth and respect. The humble seek the bounties of life they enjoy without a thought of what others think or say about it. They value freedom and independence and do not submit to the bondage of men's judgment. For the humble, ego trips are detours from the path to true success.

The humble are driven by a mission to help others. Their financial success is a byproduct of their mission to help others. The proud are driven by money. Their financial success is not a byproduct of their mission; it is their mission.

Lessons on Humility from the Life of Sam Walton

In 1962, Sam Walton opened the first Wal-Mart store at the age of 44 in Rogers, Arkansas. Five years later, in 1967, Wal-Mart had 24 stores doing more than $1 million per month in sales. In 1975, Wal-mart had 125 stores doing almost $1 million per day in sales. In 1979, Wal-Mart had 276 stores doing more than $100 million per month in sales, becoming the fastest company in history to reach a billion dollars a year in sales. Wal-Mart is now doing nearly a billion dollars a day. In 2005, Wal-Mart did $312 billion in sales from 6,200 facilities with 1.6 million employees and more than 138 million customers visiting the stores each week.[112]

Although his fame, power, and net worth grew over the years,[113] Sam Walton remained the same—a humble man focused on helping others. He "lived a clean life . . . [and was] a man whose handshake you can rely on in any kind of deal."[114] Sam

Walton saw an opportunity to bless the lives of those in small towns across America that were being overlooked by the big retail chains. He was driven by his mission "to provide a better shopping experience for everyday people living in small towns. He wanted to improve their standard of living by providing quality goods at low prices in a pleasant shopping environment."[115] Near the end of his life he said, "I have concentrated all along on building the finest retailing company that we possibly could. Period. Creating a huge personal fortune was never a goal of mine."[116]

"Even though he was a billionaire many times over, you wouldn't know it if you met him on the street. He drove [an] old pick-up truck, and he lived in a humble house in Bentonville[117] that almost anyone with a job could have afforded,"[118] and he purchased many of his clothes from Wal-Mart. "Bernard Marcus, chairman and co-founder of Home Depot, recalled going out to lunch with Walton after a meeting in Bentonville: 'I hopped into Sam's red pickup truck. No air-conditioning. Seats stained by coffee. And by the time I got to the restaurant, my shirt was soaked through and through. And that was Sam Walton—no airs [attempts to impress others], no pomposity [arrogance]."[119]

An executive who joined Wal-Mart from Frito-Lay shared this story: "After I had joined the company, I still remember seeing Sam walk into the Home Office bathroom—the same bathroom used by everybody else . . . multibillionaire Sam Walton didn't have a private executive washroom. He used the same facilities that everybody else used. This was quite a contrast for me from the executives I had known at Frito-Lay, who enjoyed a private underground parking area, private bathrooms, and an executive dining room."[120]

Don Soderquist, retired senior vice chairman of the board for Wal-Mart, shared the following experience that happened while working with Sam Walton at a store grand opening: "Like most of the grand openings, we expected a big crowd, but in this one our productivity couldn't keep up with the traffic flow. Before long, Sam jumped in and began to bag merchandise. He handed out candy to the kids and did anything he could think of to help the customers feel more comfortable with the long lines. . . I confess, as a former company president of a national retail chain and now an executive vice president for Wal-Mart, I had never served customers on the front lines like I did that day. You don't think I was going to stand around and watch my leader, do you? Sam was a very humble man, and he taught me a valuable lesson that day. None of us are too good to do the little jobs. In fact, there are no little jobs. If the chairman of the board wasn't too high and mighty to hand out lollipops and bag goods—neither was I. . . No matter how large we became, Sam always reminded us that we were no better than anyone else and should never become blinded by our own importance."[121]

Sam Walton valued Wal-Mart's employees and took the time to listen and learn from them. During his 30 years as Wal-Mart's CEO, he had a policy that any employee could contact him directly with a problem, comment, or idea. On several occasions, Sam took donuts to the Wal-Mart employees and talked to them during their breaks. He was always learning from others. In his biography he wrote, "I probably visited more headquarters' offices of more discounters than anybody else—ever. I would just show up and say, 'Hi, I'm Sam Walton from Bentonville, Arkansas. We've got a few stores out there, and I'd like to visit with Mr. So-and-So—whoever the head of the company was—about this business.' And as often as not, they'd let me in, maybe out of curiosity, and I'd ask lots of questions about pricing and distribution, whatever. I learned a lot that way."[122]

He continually tried to improve the Wal-Mart experience for the customers and employees. He wrote, "I have always [been] somebody who wants to make things work well, then better, then the best they possibly can. . . . I was never in anything for the short haul; I always wanted to build as fine a retailing organization as I could."[123]

After the company made a public stock offering in 1970, Sam implemented a profit-sharing plan for all employees to be paid in Wal-Mart stock. As a result, many managers and hourly employees retired from Wal-Mart as millionaires. Sam Walton loved each of his employees, calling them associates and treating them like family.

On April 5, 1992, at age 74, Sam Walton passed away from cancer. "The news was sent via satellite directly to the company's 1,960 stores; when the announcement played on the public address system at some stores, clerks started crying."[124] An executive of a competing store said of Sam Walton, "The way he lived his life reminded me that I had rather see a sermon than hear one anytime."[125]

ATTRIBUTE 5: HONEST

"Trust is the glue of life."

– Stephen R. Covey

CHAPTER IX

INTEGRITY PAYS

"The supreme quality for a leader is unquestionably integrity. Without it, no real success is possible."
– Dwight D. Eisenhower

In the past several years, we have seen the devastating effects of dishonest business leaders at Enron, WorldCom, Xerox, Qwest, Tyco, ImClone, Andersen, and others. They fraudulently gained short-term profits, but in the end lost everything, with many going to prison. "If you plot and connive to deceive men, you may fool them for a while, and profit thereby, but you will without fail be visited by divine punishment. To be utterly honest may have the appearance of inflexibility and self-righteousness, but in the end, such a person will receive the blessings."[126]

Honesty is key to long-term success. "A business without integrity will be penalized in the marketplace. If a business' products don't meet the claims of its advertisers, or if product quality is inconsistent, the business will lose customers to its competitors. Skilled employees, frustrated with internal policies, depart for other jobs. On the other hand, a firm known for its integrity will be rewarded by increased demand for its products and greater customer and employee loyalty."[127] "Part of the genius of an open free market system is that integrity pays. . . In the end, customers, employees, and shareholders gravitate toward companies with stable leadership—those that are credible and have integrity."[128]

When Is Success a Failure?

When unethical means are used in the pursuit of profits, success is a failure. One of Gandhi's seven sins that destroy society is "commerce without morality." It represents a moral end (commerce) achieved by an immoral means (without morality). Immoral means corrupt a worthy end into a dishonorable achievement. You cannot achieve a moral end by immoral means. Financial ends never justify unethical means.

The son of a business executive shared this story: "I grew up in a brutal business environment. My father worked as the chief executive for one of the richest men in the world, Howard Hughes, and that world turned many lives upside down. I witnessed firsthand greed, deception, power struggles, and destruction of souls all for the sake of money. But perhaps what influenced me most is what I had seen in Mr. Hughes himself. For many years on Christmas Eve or Easter Sunday, this annual ritual was not what it appeared to be; Mr. Hughes invited my father to his home. When my father arrived, Mr. Hughes would simply say, 'Bill, I just wanted to talk.' Then after a couple of hours of friendly conversation he would say, 'It's Christmas. You better get back to your family.' And I remember thinking to myself: 'With all the money, with all the power, all the accomplishments, and even all the good he has done, he is both lonely and alone.'"[129]

A dear friend and business associate of mine, G. Kent Mangelson, shared with me the following: "After nearly thirty years in the financial business and having associated with thousands of wealthy individuals, I have developed a firm philosophy about people and money. If an individual does not clearly establish personal values and goals before making financial goals, then wealth and the accumulation thereof will begin to take on a life of its own. Without clearly established values to keep the individual's direction in focus, money tends to distract the person, gradually moving him or her away from everything in life that means the most. Sadly, and all too often, when it is too late to repair the damage, the person discovers that he or she has lost those things that meant the most and that all the money in the world cannot buy nor replace that which is gone."

"In Arthur Miller's play, 'All My Sons,' a son sees his father cheating in the business world. When confronted, his dad responds, 'Son, everybody does it. You have to cheat to be successful.' The son replies, 'I know, Dad, but I thought you were better than everyone else.'"[130]

While fudging the numbers, using deceptive tactics, profiting from immoral products, and exploiting employees may be the industry standard, there is a minority who have chosen to rise above the industry standard and adhere to principles of morality and honesty in their business affairs. Our challenge is to join this minority. The business world is full of deceit and immorality, but it will only get worse unless each of us becomes an example of integrity in our work.

Jon M. Huntsman—A Billionaire the Right Way

Jon M. Huntsman was born in 1937 in the small town of Blackfoot, Idaho, to a music teacher and homemaker. Following high school, Huntsman enrolled at the Wharton School of Finance at the University of Pennsylvania. In 1961, Huntsman, age 24, graduated and went to work as a salesman for an egg-producing company and was later assigned to a team to develop a plastic egg carton. By 1967, Jon Huntsman, now age 30, was the president of Dolco Packing, a joint venture between the egg business and Dow Chemical. In 1970, Huntsman left Dolco Packing to start his own business, Huntsman Container, with his brother Blaine in Fullerton, California.

In 1971 and 1972, Huntsman worked as a special assistant to President Richard Nixon. Huntsman described an atmosphere that demanded blind loyalty to Nixon. Huntsman related the following experience, "I was asked by [H.R.] Haldeman [White House chief of staff] on one occasion to do something 'to help' the president. We were there to serve the president, after all. It seems a certain self-righteous congressman was questioning one of Nixon's nominations for agency head. There was some evidence the nominee had employed undocumented workers in her California business. Haldeman asked me to check out a factory previously owned by this congressman to see whether the report was true. The facility happened to be located close to my own manufacturing plant in Fullerton, California. . . The information would be used, of course, to embarrass the political adversary. . . There are times when we react too quickly to catch the rightness and wrongness of something immediately. We don't think it through. This was one of those times. It took about 15 minutes for my inner moral compass to . . . bring me to the point that I recognized this wasn't the right thing to do. . . Halfway through my conversation, I paused. 'Wait a minute, Jim,' I said deliberately to the general manager of Huntsman Container, 'Let's not do this. I don't want to play this game. Forget I called' . . . I informed Haldeman that I would not have my employees spy or do anything like it. To the second most powerful man in America, I was saying no. He didn't appreciate responses like that. He viewed them as a sign of disloyalty. I might as well have been saying farewell. So be it, and I did leave within six months of that incident. . . I was about the only West Wing staff member not eventually hauled before the congressional Watergate committee or grand jury."[131]

In 1974, Huntsman Container created the clamshell container for McDonald's Big Mac. Huntsman Container pioneered more than 80 innovative plastic packaging products. In 1976, Huntsman sold Huntsman container for $8 million ($28 million in 2006 dollars). As a part of the deal, Huntsman agreed to serve as CEO for four more years.

In 1982, Huntsman formed the Huntsman Chemical Corporation. Huntsman shared this story from the early years: "As our company was going through the embryonic startup years, it was necessary . . . to sell a portion of our company. I found an appropriate buyer and negotiated a price to sell. . . I agreed to sell him a 40 percent interest in our business at a fixed price. Over the next several months much delay occurred. During the process . . . our business activity quadrupled and our profits went up five-fold to the point that when it came time to sign the document, the value, instead of being $53 million was $250 million. The chairman of the company said, 'Jon, you have an important decision to make. You can either make a great deal of money from me since we have not signed anything, or you can go back to your original handshake' . . . without hesitation I was proud and honored to step up and say, 'Mr. Campan, I shook your hand. I made an agreement. The price will be $53 million. That's what we agreed to six months ago.' I must tell you that throughout the last twelve to fifteen years there have been many times I have wondered, 'What about that $200 million?' That's a fortune, a mammoth fortune. I let it slip away. And on the other hand I say, 'My children are all in the business. They know their father; they understand an agreement. If it was for $53 million or just $53, the principle is still the same. A deal is a deal. A handshake is a handshake. Integrity is integrity.'"[132]

Huntsman is an epic deal maker and powerful negotiator, but he never takes advantage of others and ensures a deal is mutually beneficial with both parties achieving their objectives. Huntsman realized that negotiating and creating deals in this manner was the right thing to do and resulted in second and third deals. Huntsman shared this example: "In 1999, I was in fierce negotiations with Charles Miller Smith, then president and CEO of Imperial Chemical Industries of Great Britain, one of that nation's largest companies. We wanted to acquire some of ICI's chemical divisions. It would be the largest deal of my life, a merger that would double the size of Huntsman Corp... During the extended negotiations, Charles' wife was suffering from terminal cancer. . . When his wife passed away, he was distraught, as one can imagine. We still had not completed our negotiations. I decided the fine points of the last 20 percent of the deal would stand as they were proposed. I probably could have clawed another $200 million out of the deal, but it would have come at the expense of Charles' emotional state. The agreement as it stood was good enough. Each side came out a winner, and I made a lifelong friend."[133]

Huntsman was the first American to own controlling interest in a business in the former Soviet Union. He founded a box company to help this emerging economy. "Initially the company was told it would have to pay a certain tax rate on boxes sold to Russian customers and a much lower rate on boxes shipped for resale to other former republics. After the company started producing boxes, a tax administrator came and informed the company that the rates were being increased on the exported boxes—to a point that made the company completely unprofitable. However, the official said, if certain amounts could be paid under the table directly to the tax official, he could 'take care of them.' It is Jon

Huntsman's policy never to pay a bribe. He never has; he never will. The official was insistent. Jon Huntsman decided to sell the factory to local management for $1 rather than pay a bribe. He lost his investment of millions of dollars, but he would not compromise his integrity for money."[134]

The first value of the Huntsman Corporation is: "We believe that ethical and moral standards are the foundation of good business policies, and we'll operate with integrity."[135] In 2005, Huntsman Corporation had 78 operations in 24 countries with 15,000 employees and company revenues of $13 billion. Huntsman is a living example that "nice guys really can and do finish first in life."[136]

ATTRIBUTE 6: OPTIMISTIC

"Optimism is the faith that leads to achievement."

– Helen Keller

CHAPTER X

SOLUTIONS OR EXCUSES

*"The world is moving so fast these days that
the man who says it can't be done is generally
interrupted by someone doing it."*
— Elbert Hubbard

Many people have been conditioned with thoughts of inadequacy. Studies have shown that within the first eighteen years of our lives, the average person is told "no" more than 148,000 times.[137] We are constantly being told by parents, friends, teachers, television, and co-workers what we cannot do. This conditioning causes many of us to achieve a small fraction of our potential. Having been conditioned this way, we often believe we can't achieve greatness, so we don't try. If we do try, we expect to fail. This result is a pessimistic approach to life. A pessimist approaches life with a statement of what can't be done instead of asking how it can be done.

To dispel the pessimist in each of us, we must transform our approach to life by finding solutions instead of excuses. I often hear people give the excuse, "I can't do it." Instead of giving an excuse, they should find a solution that begins by asking the question, "How can I do it?" Instead of saying "I can't afford it," or "It's impossible," begin asking the questions, "How can I afford it?" and "How is it possible?" This small change in our approach to life will produce great outcomes.

The Massage Chair

I was meeting with one of my business partners and financial mentors. At the time of this meeting, we were both founders and CEOs of multimillion-dollar companies. During our meeting, two deliverymen came with a massage chair for my mentor's top-floor office. The only access to the office was a narrow stairway that switched back and forth up to the office door. After a few minutes, the two deliverymen returned to let my mentor know that the chair would not fit in the office. My mentor gave a quick reply of, "Find a way to get the chair in the office." The deliveryman responded that they had done measurements and the chair would not fit. My mentor again said, "Find a way to get the chair in the office," and we continued with our meeting. The deliverymen left to make another attempt. Another few minutes went by and the deliverymen again returned saying, "There is no way for the chair to fit into your office. It is impossible."

My mentor looked at me and asked, "Will you please get the massage chair into my office?" I replied, "Absolutely," and went to work. The deliverymen were not much help. As I began to consider options to get the chair up the stairs and through the door, they said to me, "The chair will not fit, we have already tried twice." I then did measurements, to which the deliverymen said, "We already measured. It is impossible."

I calculated that if we took off the door as well as the inside molding of the doorway and went in at the right angle that it would just barely fit through the door. The deliverymen commented that it would not fit because it was impossible to get it around the switchback corner in the stairs and to hold it at the angle required to enter the door. I told them that it was possible, but it would require four people. I asked if they would help. They declined saying, "It will not fit, and what you are going to attempt will damage the chair. If you want to try it, you are on your own." My business office was close to my mentor's office, so I called over to my company and asked three of the employees to come over and help me move the chair. Once they arrived, we lifted the chair and began to maneuver it up the stairs. As we were working, the deliverymen were looking on and telling each other that we would never get the chair into the office. In a couple minutes, we had the chair up the stairs, around the corner, through the door and into the office. We had done the impossible, and had done it without damaging the chair or walls.

I thanked the three employees from my office and returned to my meeting. I entered my mentor's office and told him, "The massage chair is in your office." He replied, "We can learn a valuable lesson from what has just happened. The deliverymen came up with excuses, you came up with solutions. They said it was impossible. You said, 'How do we do the impossible?'" Then my mentor looked me in the eyes and said, "That is why they make $8 an hour and you will be a millionaire."

Winston Churchill – Courageous Optimist

"On May 10th, 1940, Winston Churchill, then age sixty-six, became Prime Minister of England. This was the time when the powerful German air force was making round-the-clock trips . . . dumping planeload after planeload of bombs on England. No one knew whether the British would be able to hold out for another week or a month."[138] "The outlook was bleak. The Nazis were running over France, Belgium, and Holland. Joseph P. Kennedy, the American ambassador in London, told Washington that Britain was finished."[139]

In the mists of the gloom and turmoil and in the face of what seemed to others like impossible odds, Churchill took office with optimism and determination. Churchill wrote of the day he took office, "I felt as though I were walking with destiny that my past life had been but a preparation for this hour for this trial . . . and I was sure I should not fail."[140]

"The key to Churchill's courage was his unbounded optimism. Only an optimist can be courageous, because courage depends on hopefulness that dangers and hazards can be overcome. . . 'I am one of those,' he remarked in 1910, 'who believe that the world is going to get better and better.' He deprecated negative thinking. In a speech to his officers in the trenches in France in 1916, Churchill exhorted: 'Laugh a little, and teach your men to laugh. . . If you can't smile, grin. If you can't grin, keep out of the way till you can.'"[141]

On May 13, 1940, Churchill gave his first speech as Prime Minister to the House of Commons. He said, "You ask, What is our aim? I can answer in one word: Victory . . . victory in spite of all the terror, victory however long and hard the road may be . . . with all the strength that God can give us. . . I take up my task with buoyancy and hope, I feel sure that our cause will not be suffered to fail."[142]

"The morning after the first night of the Blitz, Churchill drove to ground zero: London's East End and the docks. An air-raid shelter had taken a direct hit, with dozens killed and more wounded. Church's car pulled up amid the chaos. 'It was good of you to come,' the crowd called out. . . When he called out to the crowd, asking if they were disheartened, they cried back, 'No!' Churchill had come . . . to give the people the resolve they would need to face the months and years ahead."[143]

"Churchill would not permit contingency planning for failure, knowing it would inevitably leak out and breed pessimism. Just weeks after becoming Prime Minister in 1940, Churchill was advised of a doomsday plan to be implemented in the event of a full-scale German invasion of Britain. The royal family and top members of the government would be evacuated to Canada. Churchill flatly vetoed the proposal adding, 'We shall make them rue the day they try to invade our island.'"[144]

"During the last week of October 1940 . . . civilian deaths by bombing exceeded six thousands a month. In one twenty-four-hour period seven hundred aircrafts attacked Britain. . . Churchill's genius was to find a way to talk about bad news while finding hope in what others might see as defeat. . . In October of 1940 after devastating air raids, Churchill gave a speech about how the cities, 'would rise from their ruins' and blitzed homes would be rebuilt . . . When the Nazis sank vital supply ships, Churchill was there to point out that many hundreds of ships got through unscathed."[145]

Even during the worst of times, Churchill remained optimistic and confident that they would achieve victory. During a B.B.C. broadcast, Churchill proclaimed: "We are resolved to destroy Hitler and every vestige of the Nazi regime. From this, nothing will turn us—nothing. We will never parley, we will never negotiate with Hitler or any of his gang. We shall fight him by land, we shall fight him by sea, we shall fight him in the air, until, with God's help, we have rid the earth of his shadow."[146]

"Churchill not only saw reasons for hope and confidence in the darkest days of World War II but was able to infuse his unique combination of stoicism and optimism into the very backbone of the nation, the armed services, and his own staff. As Leo Amery, a minister in Churchill's government put it, 'No one ever left his cabinet without feeling a braver man.' . . . Great leaders bring out the inner strength that people often do not know they possess."[147]

On May 8, 1945, via broadcast, Churchill announced that Germany had signed the act of unconditional surrender. Churchill declared in part, "The German war is therefore at an end. . . From this Island and from our united Empire, [we] maintained the struggle single-handed for a whole year until we were joined by the military might of Soviet Russia, and . . . the United States of America. . . Finally almost the whole world was combined against the evil-doers, who are now prostrate before us. . . We must now devote all our strength and resources to the completion of our task, both at home and abroad. . . Long live the cause of freedom! . . . [We should now] give humble and reverent thanks to Almighty God for our deliverance from the threat of German domination."[148]

Churchill's determination to never give in and his optimism that victory would be achieved enabled his country to fight boldly and courageously through tremendous difficulties and also rallied the support of other countries in the cause until victory was achieved.

Churchill died on January 24, 1965. Over 300,000 people passed by his casket and millions watched the funeral proceedings via television to pay their final respects to the man who helped change the course of history. "Churchill's actions were pivotal in one of the great and most dramatic turning points of civilization. . . He knew that if he could rally the mind, spirit, and heart of the British people, they would eventually emerge victorious. . . Churchill not only saved Britain from defeat but now in retrospect, he saved democracy as a form of government in the world. Here was truly a single individual whose life made a profound difference to everyone on our planet."[149]

CHAPTER XI

UPLIFT OTHERS

"Leadership is the ability to make goodness
operate in the lives of others."
– Sterling Sill

I watch them tearing a building down,
A gang of men in a busy town,
With a ho heave ho and a lusty yell,
They swung a beam and a side wall fell
And I asked the foreman, "Are these men skilled,
The men he'd hire if he had to build?"
He gave a laugh and said, "No indeed,
Just common labor's all I need.
I can easily wreak in a day or two
What builders have taken a year to do."
I asked myself as I went my way,
Which of these roles have I tried to play.
Am I builder who works with care,
Measuring life with a rule and square?
Or am I wrecker who walks the town,
Content with the labor of tearing down.
-Author Unknown

Great achievers have learned how to uplift and inspire those around them. Your words and actions can be used to build or to destroy others. Great achievers choose to build those around them.

Studies reveal that the principles of getting along with and influencing people contribute greatly to achieving success. Teddy Roosevelt taught, "The most important single ingredient to the formula of success is knowing how to get along with people," and in Dale Carnegie's book, *How to Win Friends and Influence People*, the author writes, "Investigations revealed that even in such technical lines as engineering, about 15 percent of one's financial success is due to one's technical knowledge and about 85 percent is due to skill in human engineering—to personality and the ability to lead people." He continues, "One can, for example, hire mere technical ability in engineering, accountancy, architecture or any other profession at nominal salaries. But the person who has technical knowledge plus the ability to express ideas, to assume leadership, and to arouse enthusiasm among people—that person is headed for higher earning power. In the heyday of his activity, John D. Rockefeller said that 'the ability to deal with people is as purchasable a commodity as sugar or coffee.' And I will pay more for that ability,' said John D., 'than for any other under the sun.'"[150]

The following are 15 principles that will help you uplift others:

1. Give Sincere Compliments

People need and want to be complimented. Compliments bring out the best efforts in people by uplifting and motivating them. Even if people make mistakes, focus on their successful efforts, and compliment them on those items. The natural tendency is to tell people what they did wrong. This will result in a decrease of motivation and performance. Encouragement and compliments are a much more effective teaching device than criticism, so always look for opportunities to compliment those around you.

2. Smile

Actions speak louder than words, and a smile says, "I like you. You make me happy. I'm glad to see you." People who smile tend to manage and teach more effectively.

3. Remember Names

Remembering a person's name and using it regularly is a subtle and very effective compliment. Forget or misspell a name and you have placed yourself at a sharp disadvantage. Take the time and effort to memorize the names of each person with whom you associate. When someone tells you their name, make sure you heard it correctly. Then memorize it by repeating it in your mind, associating it with something, and when possible, write it down.[151]

4. Value Differences

To succeed with people you must value the mental, emotional, and psychological differences that exist among people. The key to valuing differences is to realize that people do not see the world as it is, but as they are. A person who is truly effective with people has the humility to recognize his own perceptual limitations and to appreciate the rich resources available through interaction with the hearts and minds of other people. Others add to your knowledge and to your understanding of reality. Is it possible for two people to disagree and both be right? Yes. For example, in a room the temperature may be 70 degrees and one individual will say it is cold while the other will say it is hot. Is the room hot or is the room cold? Which of these two individuals is right? Does one have to be right and one wrong? No, both are right from their perspective. It would be silly for the individual that was hot to tell the person who was cold that he was wrong or stupid since he thought it was cold. Until we value the differences in our perceptions and give credence to the possibility that we're both right, we will struggle in our relationships.

5. Don't Gossip

There is a tendency for people to say negative comments about those around them and to gossip about the faults of others. Don't be a part of it. If you say negative things about individuals not present, you are sending a message to those who are present that you would do the same to them. The way to gain the respect and loyalty of those present is to be respectful and loyal to those who are not present.

If constructive criticism is necessary for a specific person, it should be done in private with love and with the intent of helping the individual. Don't correct a person in front of others. Also, while giving feedback, talk about what the person does well, what you like about them, and even talk about your own mistakes before correcting theirs.

6. If Offended, Take the Initiative

Often when we are offended, our tendency is to wait for the offender to offer an apology or to at least acknowledge that he or she has wronged us. If the apology does not come, we allow our wounds to fester, and bitterness and resentment spread through our souls like poison. We then not only have a strained relationship, but a bitter soul as well. Nelson Mandela taught, "Resentment is like drinking poison and then hoping it will kill your enemies." Oftentimes, if you take the initiative to clear things up, the issue can be resolved quickly.

7. Return Good for Evil

We have a natural tendency to treat others as they treat us. Returning good for good and evil for evil is known as the law of reciprocity. This law results in either the improvement or decline of a relationship. For example, if someone is unkind to you, you respond naturally by being unkind to them. Your unkindness leads to their continued unkindness to you, and suddenly you have produced a cyclical relationship with each person returning more and more unkindness. The end result is a very unproductive and destructive relationship.

The law of reciprocity can also work in a positive direction. For example, if you show someone kindness and love, they respond naturally with kindness. This causes you to respond with even more kindness and love. This cyclical effect returns more and more kindness and love, producing a more meaningful and loving relationship. "Hatred is never ended by hatred but by love."[152]

8. Accept the Person for Who They Are

We will never fully love a person until we can accept the individual as they are. This doesn't mean we agree with or accept the person's behavior, but it does mean that our love for them is not conditional on performance or behaviors. As we increase our ability to accept the person for who they are and genuinely communicate that acceptance to them, we will increase in love for that person.

9. Tell the Individual "I Love You!"

When we genuinely communicate verbally to another person "I love you!" there is an emotional reaction heart to heart which causes each person to realize that love exists. The act is complete when the person responds genuinely back, saying, "I love you too." We increase in our ability to love through verbal expression.

10. Serve Others

When you help other people obtain their goals, you will obtain your goals. Learn to be a servant, and you will learn to be successful. It was the birthday of a mother of several children. One by one, the children began to present the gifts to their mother. It was now the youngest boy's turn. He had been given a silver platter to give to his mother. He began to approach his mother with his gift when he realized that the platter was empty. He then set the platter in front of his mother and stood upon it and said, "I give you me." Give the greatest gift you can. Give yourself.

11. Listen and Be Understanding

Our feelings and thoughts are based upon how we perceive situations, so we need to make sure we correctly understand the situation before we act. Oftentimes, when we come to understand the situation, how we feel and what we think are greatly changed.

The following story of a miscommunication between an English lady and a school master helps to illustrate this point. It seems that a little old English lady was looking for some rooms in Switzerland. She asked the local village school master to help her. A place that suited her was finally found, and the lady returned to London for her luggage. She remembered then that she had not noticed a bathroom, or as she called it, a "water closet." So she wrote to the school master. He was puzzled by the initials "W.C.," never dreaming, of course, that she was asking about a bathroom. He finally asked the help of the parish priest who decided that W.C. stood for Wesleyan Church. This was his reply:

Dear Madam,

The W.C. is situated nine miles from the house in the center of a beautiful grove of trees. It is capable of holding 350 people at a time and is open on Tuesday, Thursday and Sunday each week. A large number of folks attend during the summer months, so it is suggested you go early, although there is plenty of standing room. Some folks like to take their lunch and make a day of it, especially on Thursday when there is organ accompaniment. The acoustics are very good and everyone can hear the slightest sound.

It may be of interest to you to know that my daughter was married in our W.C. and it was there she met her husband. We hope you will be there in time for our bazaar to be held very soon. The proceeds will go towards the purchase of plush seats which the folks agree are a long-felt need, as the present seats all have holes in them. My wife is rather delicate, therefore she cannot attend regularly. It has been six months since the last time she went. Naturally, it pains her very much not to be able to go more often. I shall close now with the desire to accommodate you in every way possible and I will be happy to save you a seat down front or near the door, which ever you prefer.

-School Master

As our understanding of the situation changes, so does the message we desire to communicate.

The Need for Understanding

What would happen right now if all the air was taken out of the room you are currently in? What would happen to your interest in this book? Air is a fundamental physical need, and until that need is met, you will not be interested in anything else. However, once you have fulfilled the need for air, your interests can shift to other things. What is the emotional and psychological equivalent of air? It is the need to be understood. Why? Because when you understand another person, you fulfill many basic human needs. When you understand a person, you have accepted them. When you listen to understand a person, you are saying, "You are important and I care about you. You are a person worth listening to; a person of significance; a person that matters."

A study was done to see what people desired in a potential partner. Understanding was the number-one characteristic desired by women and the number-two characteristic desired by men. If you desire to communicate effectively with another, you must first understand them. How do we understand another? By listening. "He that answereth a matter before he heareth it, it is a folly and shame unto him."[153] Many of your problems with people will disappear and your relationships will be greatly strengthened if you will learn the simple skill of listening. As Gandhi once said, "Three-fourths of the miseries and misunderstanding in the world will disappear if we step into the shoes of our adversaries and understand their standpoint."

12. Inspire Teamwork

Napoleon Hill taught, "There is no record of anyone ever having made a great contribution to civilization without cooperation of others."[154] In order to inspire teamwork, you must be filled with enthusiasm. Enthusiasm is contagious. "Infect others with your enthusiasm, and teamwork will be the inevitable result."[155]

13. See People with an Eye of Faith

Don't treat people in terms of their behavior, but rather in terms of their potential—in terms of what they can become. Goethe put it this way, "Treat a man as he is and he will remain as he is; treat a man as he can and should be and he will become as he can and should be."

14. Be Teachable

"If we operate with the assumption that we do not have all the answers or insights, we allow ourselves to value the different viewpoints, judgments, and experiences others may bring. When we approach others with open minds, and are willing to be taught, we learn that the key to influence is to allow ourselves to be influenced."[156]

15. Give Hugs

"Hugging is healthy. It helps the immune system, cures depression, reduces stress and induces sleep. It's invigorating, rejuvenating and has no unpleasant side effects. Hugging is nothing less than a miracle drug. Hugging is an underutilized resource with magical powers."[157]

ATTRIBUTE 7: VISION

*"If we did all the things we are capable of doing,
we would literally astound ourselves."*

– Thomas Edison

CHAPTER XII

WRITE DOWN YOUR GOALS

"You are never too old to set another
goal or to dream a new dream."
– C.S. Lewis

There is great power in goals and dreams. "A study was done on Yale University's graduating class. It asked seniors a long list of questions about themselves, and three questions had to do with goals. They were: 'Do you set goals?' 'Do you write them down?' and 'Do you have an action plan to accomplish them?' Only three percent of the class answered yes to those questions. Twenty years later, a follow-up study was done. It turned out that the three percent who had said yes to goals reported that they were more happily married, were more successful in the careers they had chosen, had a more satisfactory family life, and had better health. And listen to this. Ninety-seven percent of the net worth of that graduating class was in the hands of that three percent!"[158] You have to have dreams and goals to make progress and achieve greatness. "Your progress toward success begins with a fundamental question: 'Where are you going?' Definiteness of purpose is the starting point of all achievement, and its lack is the stumbling block for ninety-eight out of every hundred people simply because they never really define their goals and start toward them. Study every person you think of who has achieved lasting success, and you will find that each one has had a definite purpose. Each had a plan for reaching that goal, and each devoted the greatest part of his or her thoughts and efforts to that end."[159]

Many people live life backwards. They take what life gives them. Many people achieve little in life simply because they never decide to achieve something. Mark Victor Hansen wrote, "It grieves me to watch individuals squander their lives because they have neglected the process of writing down their personal goals." "Most of us would like to make a positive impact on the lives of others and on our world. If we do not feel that this is in some way happening, we tend to experience a sense of emptiness, low self-worth, futility, and sometimes even depression."[160] Football coach Lou Holtz taught, "If you are bored with life, if you don't get up every morning with a burning desire to do things—you don't have enough goals."

Everyone is born with a God-given mission they are to perform. We were not sent to earth by God to be born, pay the bills and die. God sent us here for a purpose. You should define your ideal life and then go out and get it. Dreams and goals inspire us to achieve our full potential. Defining your goals and dreams will help you discover and live the purposeful, joyful, abundant life you were meant to enjoy.

The Million-Dollar Goal

> "The greater danger for most of us is not that our aim is too high and we miss it, but that it is too low and we reach it."
>
> – Michelangelo

At the end of 2000, my first business venture failed, leaving me with thousands of dollars in business debt. I was newly married and I had no income. My wife was working earning $10 per hour but her income was not even enough to cover our $1,800 a month in debt payments. I now joke with her that she married me for my money, but the truth is I had less than nothing because of the burden of debt. I was forced to put my entrepreneurial efforts on hold to look for a job. I graduated with honors from business school and applied for dozens of jobs that were a good match for my skills, experience, and degree, but I received rejection letter after rejection letter. I even applied at a call center that seemed to hire nearly everyone for a $6 per hour job and was rejected.

I now joke with people, saying, "I had to start a business because I was the only person who would hire me." In 2001, I started a new business and one of our goals was to do $1 million a year in revenue. At the time this seemed like an impossible goal, but I knew that the goal was the starting point. I knew if I did not set a goal to do $1 million in revenue with the company, then I would never figure out how to do it. I started with the goal and then every day went to work on moving the company toward this goal. The company grew and developed, and in our second year in business we achieved the goal of doing a million dollars of revenue in one year.

At this point, we set a new goal of doing a million dollars in revenue in one month, and each day I went to work to move the company toward this goal. This was another lofty goal, and it took another year of hard work and development for us to reach this goal.

It was now time for a new goal. We discussed what our new goal should be, and the idea of doing $1 million in a single day was presented. That one sounded fun and exciting, so we set the goal to do $1 million in a single day. The exciting goal was set, and now we had to figure out how to achieve it.

To go from a million dollars a year to a million dollars a month, we were able to expand and leverage what we were currently doing. To achieve the goal of doing $1 million in a single day required new approaches and models, as what we were currently doing couldn't be expanded enough to do a million dollars in revenue in a single day.

Our first opportunity to reach $1 million in a single day was in the fall of 2004 in New York City. It appeared that all the pieces were in place to do $1 million that day. The day ended, and we weren't even close to our goal. We only did $177,555 in revenue. The day was still profitable, and we were pretty happy. We learned a lot, and we saw the potential to do $1 million in a single day with a few adjustments and changes.

The next opportunity to reach our goal was in the spring of 2005 in Los Angeles. Everything was in place to do $1 million that day but would it happen? The day came and went and we again were not even close to our goal, but this time in a very, very good way. We exceeded our goal by $1.7 million—doing $2.7 million in revenue that day.

The size of your question, the size of your goals and dreams, will determine the size of your answer. If we would have never asked the question, "How do we do a $1 million in a single day?" we would have never found the answer. If you never ask the question: "How can I build a multimillion-dollar business?" "How can I become a best-selling author?" or "How can I earn a certain amount of money each year?" you will never find the answer. The goals you set will determine the type of life you build.

When you are building a house, does the house usually turn out like the blueprint? Of course it does. If you design a house to be 1,000 square feet, the house should be 1,000 square feet when you finish. Before building a house, you first ask yourself, "What kind of house would I like?" You then design the house, create a blueprint and then build the house. We should use this same process in our lives. "What kind of a life do you want? What do you want to accomplish?" Once you have determined the answers to these questions, create a blueprint for your life and follow that blueprint until you have built the life that you desire.

Walt Disney – Visionary Leader

"Of all the things I've done, the most vital is coordinating the talents of those who work for us and pointing them towards a certain goal."

– Walt Disney

Walt Disney was born in Chicago in 1901. In his youth, he discovered and fell in love with drawing and movies. In 1920, at age 18, Walt formed Iwerks-Disney Commercial Artists with Ub Iwerks. The company quickly failed, and Walt and Iwerks went to work as illustrators for the Kansas City Slide Company and there learned the basics of animation. While keeping his job at Kansas City Slide Company, Walt began creating short animated films at night. In 1922, Walt started Laugh-O-Gram Films, Inc. with $15,000 ($192,000 in 2009 dollars) from investors. Laugh-O-Gram Films, Inc. produced several short cartoons including *Little Red Riding Hood, Puss in Boots,* and *Cinderella* but struggled financially. During this time, Walt had no money for rent so he "slept on rolls of canvas and cushions at the office . . . and subsisted on cold beans he ate from a can. . . He took his baths once a week at Union Station."[161] In 1923, the company declared bankruptcy and Disney decided to leave Kansas City for Hollywood. To earn the money for the train ticket to Los Angeles, Walt spent two weeks going door-to-door in high-income areas offering to make films of their children. On his way to LA, a fellow traveler asked Walt where he was going and he replied, "I'm going to direct great Hollywood motion pictures."[162] He always had a dream.

When he arrived in Los Angeles, Walt lived with his Uncle Robert and began making the rounds to the Hollywood studios looking for a job as a director. He applied at every studio in town but was unsuccessful. With no prospects of a job, Walt, now 22 years old, requested loans from Uncle Robert and other friends to start his own studio with his brother Roy, which they called the Disney Brothers Studio. The studio received a contract to produce a series of cartoons called Alice Comedies in which a live girl named Alice had adventures in an animated world with a cat named Julius. The series was successful with the studio producing dozens of cartoons in the series. In 1926, Walt and Roy renamed the studio Walt Disney Studios. Roy said of the renaming, "It was my idea. Walt was the creative member of the team. His name deserved to be on the pictures."[163]

From 1926 to 1933 the Walt Disney Studios had several successful creations including Oswald the Lucky Rabbit, Mickey Mouse, and Three Little Pigs. "Sometime in mid-1933, at the very time he was enjoying the enormous success of Three Little Pigs, [Walt] decide that he needed to chart a new course for the studio—something big and dramatic."[164] "Walt said, 'If we were going to get anywhere, we had to get beyond the short subject. I knew that if I could crack the feature field, I could really do things'. . . Whenever Walt talked about making a feature-length animated picture, people responded, 'A cartoon is fun for seven minutes, but nobody will sit through a ninety-minute cartoon.'

Walt couldn't help wondering: Why shouldn't audiences enjoy an all-animated feature, as long as it is filled with drama, action and laughter?'"[165] "Walt Disney aimed to do something never before done in the movie industry: create a successful full-length animated feature film."[166]

One night in 1934, Walt gathered his top 40 animators and told them the story of Snow White and the Seven Dwarfs, performing the voices and actions of each of the characters. At the end of his performance, he said, "That is going to be our first feature-length film."[167]

Roy, who handled the finances of the company, estimated that the creation of *Snow White* would cost $500,000 ($7 million in 2009 dollars). When people in the industry heard that Walt was creating an animated feature film, they predicted it would be the end of the Walt Disney Studios and called the attempt "Disney's Folly." Even Walt's wife Lilly and brother Roy "tried to talk Walt out of his dream—but when they saw that he was totally committed to it, they gave up. Once Walt made a decision, no one could change his mind."[168] "[The] Walt Disney Company . . . stimulated progress throughout its history by making bold—and often risky—commitments to audacious projects."[169]

Walt Disney Studios began work on what would be a 3-year $1.5 million project ($21 million in 2009 dollars). Walt spent countless hours in a cramped projection room located under the stairwell. The room was dubbed "the sweatbox" because (as Walt put it), "There was no air conditioning and it was hot in there – plus the animators had to go in there and sweat this thing out with me."[170]

Months before the release date for *Snow White*, Walt and Roy were out of money. *Snow White* had already cost a million dollars, and a half million more was needed to complete the project. This price tag made the movie more expensive than any live action film ever produced.

Artists felt like they were working on something special, so they voluntarily donated evenings and weekends to complete the project. Meanwhile, Walt spliced what they had together to show to the head of studio loans at Bank of America, Joe Rosenberg, to seek a loan of $500,000 ($7 million in 2009 dollars) to complete the film. Joe Rosenberg liked what he saw and gave Walt the half-million dollar loan.

"Walt spent the final weeks of production ruthlessly cutting to keep the film as tight and fast-paced as possible. By the time it was completed, *Snow White* had employed more than 750 animation craftsmen. Of an estimated two million drawings created, only 250,000 actually appeared on-screen."[171]

Snow White and the Seven Dwarfs premiered in Los Angeles' 1,500-seat Carthay Circle Theatre on December 21, 1937. The Seven Dwarfs were present in full costume to greet the guests, including dozens of Hollywood's biggest stars who arrived in limousines. Surrounding the theater was a full-size replica of the dwarfs' cottage, a mill with a running waterfall, and a forest scene. An orchestra played music from the movie as search lights filled the sky. For 83 minutes, the audience was carried into a new world. The audience broke out in spontaneous applause throughout the movie, and at the conclusion Walt received a standing ovation.

In its initial release, *Snow White* earned $8.5 million ($126 million in 2009 dollars). This allowed Disney Studios to pay off its massive debt and also construct a new $3.8 million ($58 million in 2009 dollars) studio in Burbank which today continues to be the center of Disney animation.

Snow White went from "Disney's Folly" to becoming the

highest grossing film of all time, and at age 36 Walt Disney had made history. The film has been re-released several times since its first release in 1937 and has now has earned over $782 million when adjusted for inflation.[172]

Throughout his life, Walt's character was tested many times as he persevered through numerous obstacles. His resolve would again be tested as he worked to build his dream park, Disneyland. Walt wanted to create the "happiest place on earth." "He believed that by filling people's thoughts with 'happy things,' he could give them wings—wings to soar, wings to attain unbelievable heights. . . Walt envisioned people coming to Disneyland, finding happiness there, then going out and widening the circle of happiness around the world."[173]

"Once again Walt Disney's vision ran ahead of the business sense of his Hollywood colleagues. He found it difficult to find backers for the project which was slated to cost $5 million [$40 million in 2009 dollars] and eventually cost $17 million [$136 million in 2009 dollars]."[174] Since Walt did not have the support of his brother Roy and other major shareholders at Walt Disney Studios he created a new company, Walt Disney, Inc. to plan and build Disneyland. Walt spent his life savings and sold and borrowed against all his assets to launch Disneyland. In 1954, Walt purchased 160 acres of orange trees in Anaheim, CA for $800,000 ($6.4 million in 2009 dollars) to be the future site for the construction of Disneyland.[175]

John Hench, employee of The Walt Disney Company for 65 years, said, "'While we were planning Disneyland, every amusement park operator we talked to said it would fail. And Walt would come out of those meetings even happier than if they'd been optimistic'. . . They broke ground on July 12, 1954, which meant that they had to finish within a year to meet Walt's self-imposed deadline. . . [They] set themselves up in two old ranch houses on the site, where . . . the staff commandeered the kitchen, dining rooms, even closets. Walt's office was in a bedroom. There was a single bathroom in the facility."[176] Walt was continually at the construction site walking over every inch of Disneyland and directing the efforts. The park opened on July 17, 1955, with 170,000 visitors the first week and over one million visitors in the first two months.

ABC network had purchased a 34.5 percent share of Disneyland for $500,000 ($3.6 million in 2009 dollars). Five years after the opening of the park, Disney repurchased ABC's share for $7.5 million ($54 million in 2009 dollars). Once again Walt was able to bring his vision to life in spite of the doubts and predictions of failure around him.

On November 2, 1966, a large tumor was discovered in Disney's lung. The doctors told him he had 6 to 12 months to live. Disney spent his final days in a hospital beds thinking how he could best develop Disney World in Florida. He passed away 10 days after his 65th birthday on December 15, 1966. Disney had passed on but his "ability to make people happy, to bring joy to children, to create laughter and tears would not die."[177] People worldwide continue to be the beneficiaries of Walt Disney's vision. Over 500 million people have visited Disneyland since its opening in 1955, and millions watch Disney feature films each year.

Walt's oldest grandson, Chris Miller, said of Walt, "My grandfather had big dreams and goals . . . and he persevered until he achieved them. . . His life teaches all of us to believe in our dreams, to be daring in the pursuit of our goals, and to never back away from a challenge. Walt Disney was an adventurer at heart, and the way he lived is an example to us all."[178]

Walt Disney should inspire each of us to ask, "What are my big goals and dreams? What accomplishment is going to be my *Snow White*, my Disneyland? What can I do to make the world a better place?"

Questions to Help You Write Some Goals

"If you want to be happy, set a goal that commands your thoughts, liberates your energy, and inspires your hopes."
– Andrew Carnegie

Things I would like to accomplish?

Today

_____

_____

This Week

_____

_____

This Month

_____

_____

This Year

_____

_____

In the Next 5 Years

_____

_____

In the Next 10 Years

_____

_____

In the Next 20 Years

_____

_____

Before the end of my life

_____

_____

If I had 1 year to live, what would I do?

_____

_____

_____

_____

What problems in my family, community, nation, and world
most concern me? What can I do to help?

_____

_____

_____

What books will I read to help me renew and grow spiritually,
socially, intellectually, and physically?

_____

_____

_____

What would I like said about me at my funeral?

_____

_____

_____

_____

Write down the 3 people you most admire and respect and the
4 attributes you would use to describe them.

Person 1._____
    Attribute   I._____ II._____
                III._____ IV._____

Person 2. _____
    Attribute   I._____ II._____
                III._____ IV._____

Person 3. _____
    Attribute   I._____ II._____
                III._____ IV._____

What attributes do I desire to possess and exhibit? (i.e.
charitable, humble, thrifty, responsible, industrious, honest,
virtuous, etc.)

_____

_____

_____

How would I like others to describe me?

_____

_____

_____

_____

Describe my ideal life. Describe specifics. What would I do?
What would I have?

_____

_____

_____

CHAPTER XIII

VISUALIZATION AND THE WORLD'S FASTEST MAN

"What man actually needs is not a tensionless state but rather the striving and struggling for a worthwhile goal."
– Viktor E. Frankl, author of *Man's Search for Meaning*

In 1974, there was a track meet held in Tennessee with some of the greatest athletes of the day. Because of the caliber of the athletes, everyone was hoping that a new world record would be set in the 100-yard dash. One of the runners was Ivory Crockett. Before the race, the television cameras filmed Ivory Crockett folding up a little piece of paper and sticking it in his shoe. A buzz went through the crowd. Everyone was discussing why he had stuck a piece of paper in his shoe.

The starter said, "Runners, to your marks. Get set," and shot the gun. Ivory Crockett came out low with his legs churning. He had a perfect start and ran a perfect race. He pulled ahead of the pack and came across the finish line in first place. The race went so quickly that everyone was excited to see what the time would be. Had Ivory Crockett set a new world record? The official time had Ivory Crockett at 9.0—a new world record. Ivory Crockett had just run the fastest 100-yard dash in the history of the world. The crowd went wild and the press ran down to Ivory Crockett, congratulating him on the new world record. He was now "the world's fastest man." The question everybody wanted to know was what was in his shoe? Ivory Crockett sat down, unlaced his track shoes, and he pulled out of his shoe a little piece of paper. He unfolded it to the camera. It very simply read: "9.0," The *Los Angeles Times* described the event with the headline "Immortality in 9 Seconds Flat." Crockett said of setting the record, "It was a real good feeling to do something no one else had done before [and] be among the other athletes like Bob Hayes [world record holder at 9.1 seconds for 11 years] who I had revered all my life."

Read Your Goals Daily

Review your written goals daily. To help you do this, place your goals in prominent places such as your bathroom mirror, the refrigerator, the headboard of your bed, or the dashboard of your car. One of my goals is to have a #1 bestselling non-fiction book. To help me review this goal regularly, I cut out a bestseller list and pasted my book at the top of the list. I have the list with my book at the top taped to the wall right next to the light switch by my office door, so I see it every time I go in and out. Keeping your goals at the forefront of your thoughts will greatly enhance the likelihood of their achievement.

Visualization can also be used to help achieve goals. For example, let's say your goal is to get an "A" on an exam. What you visualize in relation to this goal can affect your performance. Many of us visualize the negative, so as we study, we think things such as, "I am going to forget this information" or "I am going to do poorly on the exam." Instead, visualize the positive, saying and visualizing such things as, "I will remember this information," and "I am going to do excellent on the exam."

Visualization can greatly affect performance either positively or negatively. For example, "In the early 1950s, a study was done on the effectiveness of visualization. Researchers took 90 college students with no prior basketball experience and divided those students into three groups of 30 students. Each group was told to shoot free throws and the results were recorded. For the next month, those in the first group went out and practiced shooting free throws every day. The second group was instructed to visualize shooting free throws every day, but to actually have nothing to do with a basketball. The third group was the control group and was directed to do nothing. After a month, they were again tested. The first group, as expected, had improved; they averaged a 20 percent increase in shooting accuracy. The third group, also as expected, displayed little or no improvement, shooting only 1 percent better. The big surprise was the second group; those who had practiced only in their mind improved . . . their shooting accuracy by 19 percent."[179]

A few years ago I was teaching the concept of goals and visualization at a high school when one of the girls raised her hand and said, "You talk about how goals work for businesses, but I want to go to prom. Will it work for that?"

I replied, "If that's your goal, then write it down." I then asked, "Do you know who you want to go with?" She said, "Yes." I then asked, "Can you get a picture of him?" and the audience laughed. She answered, "Yes."

I told her to put that picture on her bathroom mirror and see what happened. I then continued on with my lecture and didn't think any more about it until about a month later when I got a letter in the mail that reads:

> Mr. Taylor,
> Thank you so much for the seminar you gave at
> my high school in March. It has really inspired me

in tons of ways. Thank you. I took the advice you gave me when I asked you about how to reach my goal of going to prom. I put a picture of Mike, the boy I wanted to ask me, on my bathroom mirror, even though he had already told me he wasn't planning on going. Within a week, just like you said, my doorbell rang with an invitation to prom from Mike. We had a great time!

Thanks again,
Katie Rogerson
"prom-girl"

"One of the most powerful forces in the world is the will of men and women who believe in themselves, who dare to hope and aim high, who go confidently after the things they want from life."[180] There is great power in goals and dreams.

Create Action Plans to Achieve Your Goals

During one of the presentations I regularly give, I hold a $20 bill in the air and ask the audience, "Who wants this $20 bill?" Of course, all the hands in the room go up. I again ask, "Who wants this $20 bill?" The hands stretch a little higher and some will stand up. I continue to ask the question until someone comes up and takes the $20 from my hand. I then ask the question, "Everyone wanted the $20 bill, but who got it?" to which they reply, "The one who took action." It is the same with goals. You can write and visualize goals all you want, but if you do not take action, your goals will never become a reality. To obtain a goal you have never before achieved will require tasks you have never before done.

ATTRIBUTE 8: PERSISTENT

"Every adversity, every failure, and every heartache carries with it the seed of an equivalent or a greater benefit."

– Napoleon Hill

Chapter XIV

Success Is a Process

"Like most other overnight successes, it was
about twenty years in the making."
– Sam Walton, Founder of Wal-Mart

Many have the notion that those who are great achievers are lucky. When you study the wealthy, you will find that most did not achieve wealth by luck or by accident. One of my business partners who makes more than $1 million a year was approached by someone who said, "You are so lucky!" My partner smiled and replied, "I know, and the harder I work, the luckier I get." Thomas Edison stated, "I never did anything worth doing by accident, nor did any of my inventions come by accident; they came by work." "No one achieves anything without paying a price of hard work, integrity, emotion, and years of effort and sacrifice. It doesn't fall in your lap by luck."[181] "There is no secret to success: don't waste time looking for them. Success is the result of perfection, hard work, learning from failure, loyalty to those for whom you work, and persistence."[182]

Great achievers are not born, they are developed. If you want to make more money, have better relationships, and have a greater impact on the world, it starts with you becoming more. Success is not a process that occurs overnight. Children follow the process of learning to crawl before they walk, and learning to walk before they run. A concert pianist starts out learning to play "Chopsticks" and "Mary Had a Little Lamb." After years of practice and effort, they develop their skills to a point that they can play Beethoven's Fifth Symphony or Bach's Concertos.

Success takes time. I have never learned a principle, developed a skill, lost weight, or gained muscle in an instant. How do we go from where we are to where we want to be? In steps. "A house is built one brick at a time. Football games are won a play at a time. Every big accomplishment is a series of little accomplishments."[183] Success doesn't happen all at once. You should get better every year. Knowledge, skills, and prosperity are to be obtained by consistent and determined study and practice. There are no shortcuts to true success, so learn to work and be persistent.

$10,000/Month and the Power of a Mentor

As I neared graduation from college, I met with various mentors to decide my next step. I declined the job offers I received and declined my acceptance into one of the top MBA programs and decided to start a business. I was determined to build a multimillion-dollar company, and seeing the success of my mentors and hearing their stories gave me the hope and confidence to take the risk. I started my entrepreneurial ventures in 1999. Two years later, my business had failed and I had tens of thousands of dollars in debt. I was discouraged. I knew it was possible to build a profitable company, but I began to wonder if I would ever do it. The goal of $10,000-per-month income seemed to be impossible for me. At this point, one of my mentors who had developed a multimillion-dollar business told me this story:

> My father became a millionaire through building a business long before I did. I remember when I first

started building my business; I had a major setback on a business road trip. As I drove home, I was feeling really down and discouraged. I didn't understand why my business wasn't succeeding. I felt like I was paying the price to be successful. I was working hard and yet it seemed that everyone was succeeding but me. All I had to do was open the success and entrepreneur magazines and see every other business exploding. It seemed everyone was exploding except for me.

A couple of hours outside of my hometown, I pulled into a gas station to fill up my gas tank. I had been crying for a couple of hours at that point, so I wasn't paying attention to anything else that was happening around me. I finished filling up my tank, and put my gas cap back on. When I looked up, there stood my father, getting gas at the island across from me. I said, "Dad, what are you doing here?" He replied, "I'm out building my business." I ran over and hugged him and started crying again. Here I was, six foot three, 210 pounds and crying like a baby on my dad's shoulder.

"Dad, it's just not working for me," I cried. "I go out every day and night and work. I'm doing everything I can, but nothing is working for me." My dad then asked, "Son, do you believe I will succeed as an entrepreneur?" I replied, "You're already a multimillionaire, Dad. I know being an entrepreneur works for you. What I'm having trouble believing is that I'm ever going to be successful with my business." My dad replied, "So you believe it will work for me, but you don't believe it can work for you. But if I work with you and we work together, do you believe the business will work for us?" I replied, "Yeah,

Dad, I think it will work for us."

My dad took the lead driving home that night and for the next couple hours I followed his car and watched those two little taillights. I followed those taillights home that night and my heart felt so good to know that I had a dad, a mentor that was leading by example. I followed those taillights all the way home that night and I followed those taillights all the way to where now I am a multimillionaire. I'm so grateful to have had the taillights of mentors to follow.

My mentor then told me that his father had had struggles starting his business, but he eventually made it. Then he mentioned that he had struggled starting his own businesses and he had made it, and if I continued, I would make it, too. He then encouraged me not to give up and that success is oftentimes preceded by failures. In April 2001, I started a new business and in 2002 we did nearly a million dollars in revenue. At age 26, I achieved the goal of $10,000 income in one month for the first time, taking home $21,611 that month.

When someone is successful, don't view them as being lucky. Find out how they did it so you can achieve the same success by duplicating what they did. The quickest way to find the process to success in any field (athletics, music, finances, marriage) is to find someone who has already achieved this success and learn how they did it. Talk to people who are already where you want to be and then do what they did. If you had to walk through a minefield, would you rather follow a person who had been through the field, or learn by trial and error? Find a mentor whose footsteps you can follow to your dreams. Successful people are accessible. You simply have to seek them out. So make it a rule to get advice from people who have done what you want to do.

Anyone can be successful because everything it takes to be successful can be learned. The only thing that stands between where you are and where you want to be is time and effort. Mahatma Gandhi taught, "I claim to be no more than an average man with below-average capabilities. I have not the shadow of a doubt that any man or woman can achieve what I have if he or she would put forth the same effort and cultivate the same hope and faith."

Christopher Columbus

The Italian historian Benzoni related the following story about Christopher Columbus. After Columbus' discovery of the Americas, he was invited to a banquet where he was assigned the most honorable place at the table. He was served with ceremonials, which were observed toward kings. From across the table, a shallow courtier who was extremely jealous of Columbus abruptly asked, "If you had not discovered the Americas, would there not have been other men in Spain who would have been capable of the enterprise?" Columbus made no reply but took an egg and invited the company to make it stand on end. They all attempted the task unsuccessfully and lamented that it was impossible. He then struck the egg upon the table so as to break one end and left it standing on the broken part, illustrating that once he had shown the way to the new world, nothing was easier than to follow it. Following someone who has achieved what you want to achieve is the simplest and quickest way to get where you want to be.

Chocolate Cake Metaphor

"If someone makes the greatest chocolate cake in the world, can you produce the same quality results? Of course you can, if you have the person's recipe. A recipe is nothing but a strategy, a specific plan of what resources to use and how to use them to produce a specific result. . . So what do you need to produce the same quality cake as the expert baker? You need the recipe, and you need to follow it explicitly. If you follow the recipe to the letter, you will produce the same results, even though you may never have baked such a cake before in your life. The baker may have worked through years of trial and error before finally developing the ultimate recipe. You can save years by following his recipe, by modeling what he did. . . If you find people who already have financial success or fulfilling relationships, you just have to discover their strategy and apply it to produce similar results and save tremendous amounts of time and effort."[184]

Warren Buffett Finds a Mentor

In seeking to learn how to invest in the stock market, Warren Buffett read a book by Benjamin Graham called *The Intelligent Investor*. In this book, he found an investment philosophy and system that he could learn and apply. Warren sought Benjamin Graham as a mentor and began taking the classes Professor Graham taught at Columbia University. He even offered to work for the professor for free. In 1954, Warren Buffett was hired by Benjamin Graham to work at his New York investment firm, Graham-Newman, for $12,000 per year ($87,000 per year in 2006 dollars). Two years later, Graham retired and closed his investment firm. In 1957, Warren started his own investment partnership. His business began with seven family members and friends who invested $105,000 ($729,000 in 2006 dollars), with Warren Buffett only investing $100 ($694 in 2006 dollars) of his own money. Eleven years later in 1968, his investment partnership business was worth $104 million ($553 million in 2006 dollars). Warren Buffett continued to apply his investment strategies, and in 2006, Forbes estimated Warren Buffett's net worth to be $40 billion.

CHAPTER XV

THE POWER OF PERSISTENCE

"Persistence in spite of all obstacles, discouragement,
and impossibilities: It is this that in all things
distinguishes the strong soul from the weak."
– Thomas Carlyle

I have read the biographies of scores of great achievers. As you study their lives you find that they did not achieve their success by luck or accident, but as a result of work, persistence, and learning from their failures. A lesson everyone must learn is the need to persist when it is difficult. When we experience defeat and rejection, the easiest and most logical thing to do is to quit, but the successful have learned to persist.

Mark Victor Hansen and Jack Canfield

Before Mark Victor Hansen and Jack Canfield became the bestselling authors of the *Chicken Soup for the Soul* series, which has now sold over 100 million copies, they were rejected by 140 publishers and told by their agent, "I can't sell this book—I'm giving it back to you guys."

The Wright Brothers

Before the Wright brothers became the inventors of modern aviation, they had thousands of failed experiments and glides.

Orville Wright wrote, "Our first experiments were rather disappointing. The machine . . . at times seemed to be entirely beyond control."[185]

Stephen R. Covey

Stephen R. Covey, author of *The Seven Habits of Highly Effective People*, created one of the largest leadership development companies in the world. Before the company was worth $160 million, the company endured 11 straight years of negative cash flow. The company had nothing in the bank, they were totally extended on their accounts payable, and their credit lines were maxed out. Their "debt to tangible net worth" ratio was 223 to 1. Over the next two and a half years, the company value grew to a worth of $160 million.[186]

Sam Walton

Before Sam Walton founded Wal-Mart, he lost his first store, a Ben Franklin variety store, after 5 years of hard work. Sam Walton wrote of the experience, "It was the low point of my business life. I felt sick to my stomach. I couldn't believe it was happening to me. It really was a nightmare. I had built the best variety store in the whole region and worked hard in the community—done everything right—and now I was being kicked out of town. It didn't seem fair. . . I've always thought of problems as challenges, and this one wasn't any different. . . The challenge at hand was simple enough to figure out: I had to pick myself up and get on with it, do it all over again, only even better this time. . . I had a chance for a brand-new start, and this time I knew what I was doing."[187] The next store he opened was Wal-Mart.

Walt Disney

Walt Disney suffered a devastating setback in 1928—a blow so harsh that his career seemed about to disintegrate. He lost his first successful cartoon creation, Oswald the Lucky Rabbit, because he had naively signed away the ownership rights. Emerging empty-handed from the debacle, Disney didn't quit. He continued to work, and his next creation was Mickey Mouse.[188]

Sylvester Stallone

Before Sylvester Stallone was a famous writer and actor, he was rejected by over 600 casting agents and was unable to sell his first 8 screenplays. In 1975, Stallone saw a fight between Muhammad Ali and Chuck Wepner in which Wepner was a 30:1 underdog. Inspired by this fight, Stallone began developing the *Rocky* screenplay. The script was purchased by United Artists and opened in theaters on November 21, 1976. Rocky took in $117 million ($389 million in 2006 dollars) in U.S. box office sales, with Stallone making more than $5 million ($16.6 million in 2006 dollars).

Christopher Columbus

Before Christopher Columbus was recognized as one of the greatest explorers, he was rejected by numerous people for 20 years until finally Queen Isabella and King Ferdinand agreed to support his venture. Columbus wrote of his struggle, "Those who heard of my [adventurous enterprise] called it foolish, mocked me, and laughed."[189] On the evening of August 3, 1492, Columbus left from Spain with three ships, the *Niña*, *Pinta*, and *Santa Maria*. On October 10, 1492, 68 days after leaving Spain, Columbus' crew began to lose hope of ever reaching their destination. Frightened that they would die at sea, his officers and crew demanded that they turn back and return to Spain. Columbus' crew threatened to kill him if he did not consent to their request. Columbus urged them to reconsider and proposed a compromise. Columbus suggested that if land was not found after two more days, they would turn back. The officers and crew accepted the compromise. On October 11, they spotted land birds and other signs of nearing land and at 2 a.m. ". . . on October 12th, with the Pinta sailing ahead, the weather cleared. In the moonlight one of the sailors on the Pinta, Juan Rodriquez Bermejo, saw a white sand beach and land beyond it. After his shout of 'Land! Land!' the Pinta's crew raised a flag on its highest mast and fired a cannon."[190] Columbus achieved a grand victory because he had the courage to press forward when all others had lost faith.

Colonel Sanders

Before Kentucky Fried Chicken (KFC) was one of the world's largest restaurants, Colonel Sanders was rejected over 1,000 times. In the early 1950s, Colonel Harland Sanders was forced to sell his restaurant as a result of an interstate highway that bypassed Corbin, Kentucky, and reduced the number of customers who came to his restaurant. At age 65, Colonel Sanders was reduced to living on his Social Security check of $105 per month ($791 per month in 2006 dollars).

While running his restaurant, he had perfected a recipe and cooking technique for fried chicken. Confident of the quality of his fried chicken, he decided to try and sell his recipe and cooking techniques. He drove all across the country from restaurant to restaurant cooking batches of chicken for restaurant owners and their employees. He was rejected 1,009 times before he found someone willing to purchase his recipe.[191] Colonel Sanders persisted through hundreds of rejections until he got a "yes."

After his first "yes," his franchising idea began to take off. To those who agreed to buy his recipe, he entered into a handshake agreement that stipulated payment to him of a nickel (36 cents in 2006 dollars) for each chicken the restaurant sold. By 1964, at age 74, Colonel Sanders had more than 600 franchised outlets for his chicken in the United States and Canada.

Colonel Sanders said of the beginning days, "I hand-mixed the spices in those days like mixing cement on a specially cleaned concrete floor on my back porch in Corbin. I used a scoop to make a tunnel in the flour and then carefully mixed in the herbs and spices. My wife, Claudia, was my packing girl, my warehouse supervisor, my delivery person—you name it. Our garage was the warehouse. After I hit the road selling franchises for my chicken, that left Claudia behind to fill the orders for the seasoned flour mix. She'd fill the orders in little paper sacks with cellophane linings and package them for shipment. Then she had to put them on a midnight train." In 1964, Colonel Sanders sold his interest in the U.S. company for $2 million ($13 million in 2006 dollars) but remained the public spokesman for the company. KFC continued to grow and now does billions in sales each year and serves millions of customers daily in over 13,000 restaurants in 80 countries.

Cameron C. Taylor

Before I was a published author, I struggled to write. Prior to my first semester at college, I set a goal to become a published author. I remember receiving my first writing assignment and being so excited to begin my writing career. I worked hard on this paper, spending dozens of hours ensuring it was my best effort and an "A" paper. A couple weeks after the papers were turned in, I remember the teacher starting class by putting on the board the grades "A" through "F" and the break down of how the members of the class scored on the paper. I was sure I had turned in one of the "A" papers. I was going to be a published author and I had worked so hard on the paper. Well, I got my paper handed back to me and on the top of the paper was not an "A," "B," or "C," and it wasn't even a "D." On top of my paper was written "F" with the note, "This is not collegiate material. You need help. Get a tutor." This was the start of my writing career. Writing had been one of my worst subjects in high school, but I was determined to make it one of my best. I went to the teacher and asked if he would give me a list of the students that got an "A" on the paper so I could see what an "A" paper looked like and learn from them. I began to take writing classes and to learn from other authors. I worked hard to improve and develop my writing skills, and by my senior year I was a published author. My first book was published by the college for use in one of the university's leadership courses.

Conclusion

Abraham Lincoln taught, "Always bear in mind that your own resolution to succeed is more important than any other."[192] There are no failures in life, only those who quit before success. Failure is a part of learning. The formula for success is trying until you succeed. If you give up during the struggle, you will never experience the victory.

CONCLUSION

LESSONS LEARNED FROM THE SCRATCHED FERRARI

I volunteer as the Scout Master in our local troop. Our troop was creating a movie to earn the cinematography merit badge, and we needed to film one of the scenes with a luxury car. One of my neighbors has two beautiful Ferraris, so I arranged with him to film this scene at his home.

My five-year-old son came with me for the filming and was to have a part in the scene as an elf. We were in my neighbor's garage, and he was showing me the pictures on his "wall of fame and shame (crashes)" of his various vehicles. As we were looking at the pictures, we heard a crash and turned around to see a chair on the front of the red Ferrari. In front of the Ferrari was a raised workbench area with a chair on wheels. My son had accidentally knocked the chair off the workbench platform onto the hood of the Ferrari.

Lesson 1 – The Root of Our Actions Is Our Attributes

C.S. Lewis taught, "Surely what a man does when he is taken off his guard is the best evidence for what sort of a man he is? Surely what pops out before the man has time to put on a disguise is the truth? If there are rats in a cellar you are most likely to see them if you go in very suddenly. But the suddenness does not create the rats; it only prevents them from hiding. In the same way the suddenness of the provocation does not make me an ill-tempered man: it only shows me what an ill-tempered man I am."[193]

A chair damaging my neighbor's Ferrari definitely caught both me and my neighbor off guard and would certainly classify as a sudden provocation. My son ran and hid behind one of our friends who was with us, who later told me my son's heart was beating extremely fast as he waited to see what would happen next. I was quite impressed by my neighbor's reaction. He remained calm and said to my son, "That is why they make paint; I will be able to have it fixed." From my interaction with this neighbor, my impressions were that he was a wonderful and kind man. To see that his immediate reaction was one of patience, love, and concern for my son illustrated that my neighbor truly was a man who had the attributes of love, caring, and patience to his very core.

The key to changing how we act and live is to change the attributes we possess. Often people try to correct behavior when behavior is not the real problem. In the words of Henry David Thoreau, "There are a thousand hacking at the branches of evil to one who is striking at the root."[194] Our behaviors stem from the attributes we possess. Thus, if we want to make lasting change and improvements in our lives, we need to develop the attributes that lead to the behavior and life we desire.

Lesson 2 – Attributes Can Be Developed

When we arrived home after filming, I told Mitchell that even though it was an accident, he was still responsible for the damage that he had caused to our neighbor's Ferrari, and he needed to give all the money he had worked for over the last several months to our neighbor to help pay for the repair. My son didn't like this idea and began to cry, saying, "I don't want to lose all my money. I will have to start all over." I explained to him that when we damage something that is not ours we have the responsibility and duty to pay to repair the damage. His crying continued as I had him take all the dollars and coins out of his savings jar and put them in an envelope for me to take to our neighbor. I returned to my neighbor's home with an envelope containing my son's money and a blank check from me payable to him to have the Ferrari repaired.

As I write this I am reminded of incidences from the life of Abraham Lincoln, who on multiple occasions repaid debt and met financial obligations under severe distress. One of these incidences occurred in 1837, when Lincoln and others had incurred a large financial obligation. Many of those who owed the obligation were impoverished from the Panic of 1837 and none of the debtors were flourishing. Some sought to be relieved of the burden by seeking a legislative amendment which would have removed the obligation, but Lincoln objected to such action saying, "We have the benefit. Let us stand to our obligations like men." These were trying times for each of those repaying the debt, and at this time Abraham Lincoln's financial condition was described as worse than penniless because of the burden of debt upon him. At times, he was unable to supply even his most pressing needs. Great sacrifices were made to make the payments and repay the debt, and finally, after 8 long years, the debt was paid in full. The painfully liquidated note is now framed and displayed in a banking house at Springfield where all who enter may see. It serves as a memorial to the rectitude of the community during those trying times.[195]

Each of the attributes of great achievers can be developed. My son having to pay for damaging the Ferrari and this story from Lincoln will help my son develop the attribute of being responsible so that he will "stand to his obligations like a man."

To achieve the attributes of great achievers requires more than knowledge and belief. Gandhi once said, "There are 999 who believe in honesty for every honest man." For the principle of honesty to really impact your life, it must become more than something you know—it must be something you are. You can't just know about honesty and believe it is a true principle. You must be an honest person. It must be a part of you—it must be an attribute you possess. May we each spend the time in study and practice to develop and live the attributes of great achievers.

The 8 Attributes of Great Achievers

Attribute 1: Responsible

Attribute 2: Creator

Attribute 3: Independent

Attribute 4: Humble

Attribute 5: Honest

Attribute 6: Optimistic

Attribute 7: Vision

Attribute 8: Persistent

I hope that this book has been enjoyable and helpful to you. I would love to hear from you. Please tell me what you enjoyed about the book and how it has impacted your life.

Cameron C. Taylor

428 E. Thunderbird Road #504

Phoenix, AZ 85022

CameronTaylor@DoesYourBagHaveHoles.org

ENDNOTES

1   Michael and Jana Novak, *Washington's God* (Basic Books, 2006) p. 8.
2   Benjamin Franklin, *The Autobiography of Benjamin Franklin* (Philadelphia: Henry Altemus, 1895) p. 150-154.
3   Jim Collin, *Good to Great* (New York: Harper Collins, 2001) p. 51.
4   Charles Hockema.
5   The story from the beginning to the start of the conversation with the prison guard is an account from my memory of an experience I had teaching at a prison. The conversation with the prison guard to the end of the story is based on two true stories from the lives of two of my mentors. I felt the principles taught by these stories could best be told in the context of the prison encounter. Thus, from the prison guard to the conclusion of the story is fictional but is based on two true stories.
6   Viktor E. Frankl, *Man's Search for Meaning* (New York: Pocket Books, 1984) p. 178.
7   Viktor E. Frankl, *Man's Search for Meaning* (New York: Pocket Books, 1984) p. 178.
8   Stephen R. Covey, *The Seven Habits of Highly Effective People* (New York: Simon & Schuster, 1989) p. 69-70.
9   George G. Ritchie with Elizabeth Sherrill, *Return from Tomorrow* (Grand Rapids, MI: Fleming H. Revell, 1978) p. 115.
10 George G. Ritchie with Elizabeth Sherrill, *Return from Tomorrow* (Grand Rapids, MI: Fleming H. Revell, 1978) p. 115-116.
11 Steve Young, *Steve Young's Hall of Fame Send Off*, July 30, 2005.
12 Saundra Davis Westervelt, *Shifting the Blame* (New Brunswick, NJ: Rutgers University Press, 1998) p. 4, 7.
13 Thomas S. Monson, "In Search of an Abundant Life," *Tambuli*, Aug. 1988, p. 3.
14 Eknath Easwaran, *Gandhi the Man* (Nilgiri Press, 1997) p. 11.
15 Eknath Easwaran, *Gandhi the Man* (Nilgiri Press, 1997) p. 17.
16 Eknath Easwaran, *Gandhi the Man* (Nilgiri Press, 1997) p. 20.
17 Blaine Lee, *The Power Principle* (New York: Simon & Schuster, 1997) p. 170-171.
18 Lance H. K. Secretan, *Inspire! What Great Leaders Do* (Hoboken, NJ: Wiley 2004) p. 67.
19 Gandhi.
20 Anna Craft, Howard Gardner, Guy Claxton, *Creativity, Wisdom, and Trusteeship* (Thousand Oaks, CA: Corwin Press, 2007) p. 90.
21 Aldous Huxley.
22 Keshavan Nair, *A Higher Standard of Leadership* (San Francisco: Berrett-Koehler Publishers, Inc., 1997) p. 63.
23 Eknath Easwaran, *Gandhi the Man* (Nilgiri Press, 1997) p. 47.
24 Buddha cited in Sue Patton Thoele, *Growing Hope* (Yorkbeach, ME: Red Wheel/Weiser, 2004) p. 148
25 Gandhi.
26 Eknath Easwaran, *Gandhi the Man* (Nilgiri Press, 1997) p. 49, 56.
27 M.V. Vamath, Gandhi, *A Spiritual Journey* (Mumbai, India: Indus Source Books, 2007) p. 77.
28 Jafar Mahmud, *Mahatma Gandhi* (New Delhi: A.P.H. Publishing, 2004) p. 25.
29 Keshavan Nair, *A Higher Standard of Leadership* (San Francisco: Berrett-Koehler Publishers, Inc., 1997) p. 59.
30 Catherine Bush, *Gandhi* (New York: Chelsea House Publishers, 1985) p. 98.
31 Keshavan Nair, *A Higher Standard of Leadership* (San Francisco: Berrett-Koehler Publishers, Inc., 1997) p. 2.
32 Don Soderquist, *Live Learn Lead to Make a Difference* (Nashville, TN: J. Countryman, 2006) p. 9.
33 Stephen Budiansky, "10 Billion for Dinner, Please," *U.S. News & World Report,* 12 September 1994, p. 57-62.

34   Paul Pilzer, *God Wants You to Be Rich* (New York: Simon & Schuster, 1995) p. 18–19.
35   Stephen R. Covey, *Principle-Centered Leadership* (New York: Simon & Schuster, 1991) p. 159.
36   The overall story is fictional, but is based on several true stories.
37   Hyrum Smith, *The 10 Natural Laws of Successful Time and Life Management* (New York: Warner Books, 1994) p. 201–202.
38   Harold C. Livesay, *American Made* (New York: Pearson Longman, 2007) p. 269.
39   Bureau of Economic Analysis, U.S. Department of Commerce, Regional Economic Accounts, State Quarterly Personal Income, SQ1-Personal Income.
40   U.S. Department of Transportation, Federal Highway Administration, Exhibit 1.1 National Summary Statistics: 1960–2000.
41   Introductory Note, Benjamin Franklin, *The Autobiography of Benjamin Franklin* (Dover Publications, Inc., 1996) p. iii.
42   Benjamin Franklin, *The Autobiography of Benjamin Franklin* (New York: The MacMillan Company, 1921) p. 11.
43   Walter Isaacson, *Benjamin Franklin* (New York: Simon & Schuster, 2003) p. 94.
44   Edited by E. Boyd Smith, Benjamin Franklin, *The Autobiography of Benjamin Franklin* (New York: Henry Holt and Company, 1916) p. 169-170.
45   Walter Isaacson, *Benjamin Franklin* (New York: Simon & Schuster, 2003) p. 100.
46   Edited by E. Boyd Smith, Benjamin Franklin, *The Autobiography of Benjamin Franklin* (New York: Henry Holt and Company, 1916) p. 113.
47   Edited by E. Boyd Smith, Benjamin Franklin, *The Autobiography of Benjamin Franklin* (New York: Henry Holt and Company, 1916) p. 119.
48   Walter Isaacson, *Benjamin Franklin* (New York: Simon & Schuster, 2003) p. 72.
49   Clark DeLeon, "Divvying up Ben: Let's Try for 200 More", *Philadelphia Inquirer*, February 7, 1993, page B02.
50   Benjamin Franklin, *Essays and Letters, Volume 1* (New York: R. & W.A. Barton & Co., 1821) p. 91.
51   Lynn G. Robbins, *Uncommon Cents* (Salt Lake City, UT: Leather Bound Books, 2004) p. 13.
52   Benjamin Franklin, *Essays and Letters Volume 1*, (New York: R. & W.A. Barton & Co., 1821) p. 92–94.
53   Walter Isaacson, *Benjamin Franklin* (New York: Simon & Schuster, 2003) p. 130.
54   Leon J. Cole, *The Delta of the St. Clair River*, (Lansing, MI: Robert Smith Printing Company, 1903) p. 196.
55   Leon J. Cole, *The Delta of the St. Clair River* (Lansing, MI: Robert Smith Printing Company, 1903) p. 197.
56   Edited by E. Boyd Smith, Benjamin Franklin *The Autobiography of Benjamin Franklin*, (New York: Henry Holt and Company, 1916) p. 289-290.
57   Edited by Albert Henry Smyth; Benjamin Franklin, *The Writings of Benjamin Franklin, Volume II*, (New York: The MacMillan Company, 1905) p. 325.
58   Edited by Albert Henry Smyth; Benjamin Franklin, *The Writings of Benjamin Franklin, Volume II* (New York: The MacMillan Company, 1905) p. 410.
59   Walter Isaacson, *Benjamin Franklin* (New York: Simon & Schuster, 2003) p. 137.
60   Benjamin Franklin, *Memoirs of the Life and Writings of Benjamin Franklin* (London: Printed for Henry Colburn, British and Foreign Public Library, 1818) p. 372.
61   Walter Isaacson, *Benjamin Franklin* (New York: Simon & Schuster, 2003) p. 143, 145.
62   Edited by E. Boyd Smith, Benjamin Franklin, *The Autobiography of Benjamin Franklin* (New York: Henry Holt and Company, 1916) p. 115.
63   Edited by E. Boyd Smith, Benjamin Franklin, *The Autobiography of Benjamin Franklin* (New York: Henry Holt and Company, 1916) p. 136.

64   University of Pennsylvania, retrieved 9-24-2009 from
     http://www.upenn.edu/about/heritage.php.

65   Edited by Jared Sparks, *The Works of Benjamin Franklin, Volume 1* (Boston: Whittemore,
     Niles, and Hall, 1856) p. 569, 576.

66   Walter Isaacson, *Benjamin Franklin* (New York: Simon & Schuster, 2003) p. 147.

67   *Some Account of the Pennsylvania Hospital; From Its First Rise, to the Beginning of the
     Fifth Month, Called May, 1754* (Philadelphia: Printed at the Office of the United States'
     Gazetter, 1817) p. 33.

68   University of Pennsylvania, retrieved 9-24-2009 from
     http://www.uphs.upenn.edu/paharc/timeline/1751/tline1.html.

69   Edited by E. Boyd Smith, Benjamin Franklin, *The Autobiography of Benjamin Franklin*
     (New York: Henry Holt and Company, 1916) p. 228.

70   University of Pennsylvania, retrieved 9-24-2009 from
     http://www.pennhealth.com/pahosp/about/.

71   PBS, retrieved 9-24-2009 from http://www.pbs.org/benfranklin/l3_citizen_founding.html.

72   Jared Sparks, *The Life of Benjamin Franklin* (Boston: Whittemore, Niles and Hall) p. 408.

73   PBS, retrieved 9-24-2009 from http://www.pbs.org/benfranklin/l3_citizen_founding.html.

74   The Paris Peace Treaty (1783).

75   PBS, retrieved 9-24-2009 from http://www.pbs.org/benfranklin/l3_citizen_founding.html.

76   Edited by E. H. Scott; James Madison, *Journal of the Federal Convention* (Chicago: Scott,
     Foresman and Co., 1898) p. 741-743.

77   George Ticknor Curtis, *Constitutional History of the United States Volume I* (New York:
     Harper & Brothers, Franklin Square, 1889) p. 294.

78   Independence Hall Association, Retrieved September 26, 2009 from
     http://www.ushistory.org/franklin/philadelphia/grave.htm.

79   Abraham Lincoln, *Life and Works of Abraham Lincoln, Volume V* (New York: The Current
     Literature Publishing Co., 1907) p. 67–68, 186.

80   Fred G. Gosman, *Spoiled Rotten* (New York: Villard, 1992) p. 32.

81   Thomas J. Stanley, William D. Danko, *The Millionaire Next Door* (New York: Simon &
     Schuster, 1996) p. 142–143.

82   Barbara Hagenbaugh, "More Than Half of Teens Forgo Summer Jobs," *USA Today*, July 9,
     2007.

83   Roberta Rand, "When Adult Children Move Back Home," *Focus on the Family.*

84   Sheila J. Curran, "The Adult-Child Comes Homes," *Duke University News*, July 21, 2006.

85   Elbert Hubbard, *Love, Life & Work* (The Roycrofters, 1906) p. 84.

86   "What was the Coast Guard's role in the world's first heavier than air flight, made by the
     Wright Brothers on 17 December 1903?" *United States Coast Guard.* Retrieved December
     8, 2006, from http://www.uscg.mil/history/faqs/Wright_Brothers.html.

87   Fred C. Kelly, *The Wright Brothers* (Mineola, NY: Dover Publications, 1989) p. 8.

88   "The Unlikely Inventors," *Public Broadcasting Service (PBS).* Retrieved December 11,
     2006, from http://www.pbs.org/wgbh/nova/wright/inventors.html.

89   *Academic American Encyclopedia* (Princeton, NJ: Arete Publishing Co., 1980) p. 212.

90   "Wright Brothers," *Wikipedia.* Retrieved December 7, 2006, from
     http://en.wikipedia.org/wiki/Wright_brothers.

91   Tom D. Crouch, *The Bishop's Boys* (New York: W. W. Norton & Company, 1989) p.
     273–274.

92   Tom D. Crouch, *The Bishop's Boys* (New York: W. W. Norton & Company, 1989) p. 429.

93   Tom D. Crouch, *The Bishop's Boys* (New York: W. W. Norton & Company, 1989) p. 429.

94   Fred Howard, *Wilbur and Orville* (New York: Alfred A. Knopf, 1987) p. 16.

95   Judith A. Dempsey, *A Tale of Two Brothers* (Victoria, BC, Canada: Trafford Publishing,
     2003) p. 26.

96   Tom D. Crouch, *The Bishop's Boys* (New York: W. W. Norton & Company, 1989) p. 12.

97   Louise Borden and Trish Marx, *Touching the Sky* (New York: Margaret K. McElderry Books, 2003).

98   Tom D. Crouch, *The Bishop's Boys* (New York: W. W. Norton & Company, 1989) p. 465–466.

99   Don Soderquist, *Live Learn Lead to Make a Difference* (Nashville, TN: J. Countryman, 2006) p. 92–93.

100   Edwin A. Locke, *The Essence of Leadership* (New York: Lexington Book, 1991) p. 79.

101   Complied by Rev. Frederick S. Sill, *A Year Book of Colonial Times* (New York: E.P. Dutton and Company, 1906) p. 15.

102   Thomas J. Stanley, William D. Danko, *The Millionaire Next Door* (New York: Simon & Schuster, 1996) p. 48, 71.

103   Joseph Addison, *The Works of Joseph Addison, Volume III* (New York: Harper & Brothers Publishers, 1864) p. 42.

104   Burke Hedges, *Read & Grow Rich* (Tampa, FL: INTI Publishing, 2000) p. 3.

105   Socrates. *Wikiquote*. Retrieved January 1, 2007, from http://en.wikiquote.org/wiki/Socrates.

106   *Publishers Weekly*, September 18, 2006, p. 4.

107   Mark Twain. *Wikiquote*. Retrieved January 1, 2007, from http://en.wikiquote.org/wiki/Mark_Twain.

108   Robert Kiyosaki, *Rich Dad, Poor Dad*, (Paradise Valley, AZ: TechPress, Inc., 1998) p. 152.

109   Alvin Toffler cited in Jarvis Finger, Neil Flanagan, *The Management Bible* (London: New Holland Publishers, 2006) p. xv.

110   B.J. Losing, *Signers of the Declaration of Independence* (New York: George F. Colledge & Brother, 1848) p. 167.

111   Blaine Lee, *The Power Principle* (New York: Simon & Schuster, 1997) p. 132.

112   *Wal-Mart*, retrieved January 8, 2007, from http://www.walmartfacts.com/content/default.aspx?id=3.

113   In 1985, Sam Walton became the wealthiest man in America with a net worth of $2.8 billion ($5.1 billion in 2006 dollars). At his death in 1992, Sam's net worth was estimated at $28 billion. He left his ownership in Wal-Mart to his wife and four children whose combined net worth in 2005 was approximately $80 billion.

114   Vance H. Trimble, *Sam Walton* (New York: Dutton, 1990) p. 6–8.

115   Don Soderquist, *Live Learn Lead to Make a Difference* (Nashville, TN: J. Countryman, 2006) p. 121.

116   Sam Walton, *Sam Walton* (New York: Doubleday, 1992) p. 234.

117   Bentonville, AK, had a population of 11,257 at the 1990 census.

118   Michael Bergdahl, *What I Learned From Sam Walton* (New York: John Wiley & Sons, 2004) p. 114.

119   Daniel Gross, *Forbes Greatest Business Stories of All Times* (New York: John Wiley & Sons, 1996) p. 274.

120   Michael Bergdahl, *What I Learned From Sam Walton* (New York: John Wiley & Sons, 2004) p. 132.

121   Don Soderquist, *Live Learn Lead to Make a Difference* (Nashville, TN: J. Countryman, 2006) p. 44–45.

122   Sam Walton, *Sam Walton* (New York: Doubleday, 1992) p. 81.

123   Sam Walton, *Sam Walton* (New York: Doubleday, 1992) p. 78-79.

124   Daniel Gross, *Forbes Greatest Business Stories of All Times* (New York: John Wiley & Sons, 1996) p. 283.

125   Daniel Gross, *Forbes Greatest Business Stories of All Times* (New York: John Wiley & Sons, 1996) p. 270.

126 John Breen, Mark Teeuwen, *Shinto in History* (Honolulu: University of Hawaii Press, 2000) p. 169.

127 Jay Van Andel, *An Enterprising Life* (New York: Harper Collins, 1998) p. 53–54

128 Kevin Rollins, Former President/CEO of Dell.

129 Robert C. Gay, *Business with Integrity* (Provo, UT: Brigham Young University Press, 2005) p. 49.

130 W. Steve Albrecht, *Business with Integrity* (Provo, UT: Brigham Young University Press, 2005) p. 5–6.

131 Jon M. Huntsman, *Winners Never Cheat* (Upper Saddle River, NJ: Wharton School Publishing, 2005) p. 9–11.

132 Jon M. Huntsman, Sr., *Business with Integrity* (Provo, UT: Brigham Young University Press, 2005) p. 91–92.

133 Jon M. Huntsman, *Winners Never Cheat* (Upper Saddle River, NJ: Wharton School Publishing, 2005) p. 40–41.

134 Ned C. Hill, *Business with Integrity* (Provo, UT: Brigham Young University Press, 2005) p. 79–80.

135 Mission and Values, *Huntsman International*, Retrieved January 18, 2007, from http://www.huntsman.com/index.cfm?PageID=831.

136 Jon M. Huntsman, *Winners Never Cheat* (Upper Saddle River, NJ: Wharton School Publishing, 2005) p. 9.

137 Shad Helmstetter, *What to Say When You Talk to Your Self* (New York: Pocket Books, 1986) p. 20.

138 Sterling W. Sill and Dan McCormick, *Lessons from Great Lives* (Aylesbury Publishing, 2007) p. 31.

139 Celia Sandys and Jonathan Littman, *We Shall Not Fail* (New York: Portfolio, 2003) p. 3.

140 Winston Churchill, *The Second World War, Volume I, The Gathering Storm* (New York: Houghton Mifflin Company, 1948) p. 601.

141 Steven F. Hayward, *Churchill on Leadership* (New York: Gramercy Books, 2004) p. 115.

142 Winston Churchill, *The Second World War, Volume II, Their Finest Hour* (New York: Houghton Mifflin Company, 1949) p. 24.

143 Celia Sandys and Jonathan Littman, *We Shall Not Fail* (New York: Portfolio, 2003) p. 174-175.

144 Celia Sandys and Jonathan Littman, *We Shall Not Fail* (New York: Portfolio, 2003) p. 151.

145 Celia Sandys and Jonathan Littman, *We Shall Not Fail* (New York: Portfolio, 2003) p. 249, 179-180.

146 Winston Churchill, *The Second World War, Volume III, The Grand Alliance* (New York: Houghton Mifflin Company, 1950) p. 332.

147 Celia Sandys and Jonathan Littman, *We Shall Not Fail* (New York: Portfolio, 2003) p. 173-174.

148 Winston Spencer Churchill, *Never Give In! The Best of Winston Churchill's Speeches* (New York, Hyperion, 2003) p. 389-390.

149 Hyrum W. Smith, *What Matters Most* (New York: Simon & Schuster, 2000) p. 33-37.

150 Dale Carnegie, *How to Win Friends and Influence People* (New York: Pocket Books, 1982) p. xiv.

151 Dale Carnegie, *How to Win Friends and Influence People* (New York: Pocket Books, 1982) p. 75-83.

152 Buddha.

153 Proverbs 18:13, King James Version.

154 Napoleon Hill, *Napoleon Hill's Keys to Success* (New York: Plume, 1997) p. 154.

155 Napoleon Hill, *Napoleon Hill's Keys to Success* (New York: Plume, 1997) p. 155.

156 Blain Lee, *The Power Principle* (New York: Simon & Schuster, 1997) p. 132.

157 Jack Canfield and Mark Victor Hansen, *Chicken Soup for the Soul* (Deerfield Beach, FL: Health Communications 1993) p. 17-18.

158 Lou Tice, *Personal Coaching for Results* (Nashville: Nelson, 1997) p. 93.

159 Napoleon Hill, *Keys to Success* (New York: Penguin, 1994) p. 1.

160 Neal Gabler, *Walt Disney* (New York: Alfred A. Knopf, 2006) p. 71.

161 Marc Eliot, *Walt Disney* (Andre Deutsch Ltd, 1995) p. 23.

162 Bob Thomas, *Building a Company: Roy O. Disney and the Creation of an Entertainment Empire* (New York: Hyperion, 1998) p. 53.

163 Neal Gabler, *Walt Disney* (New York: Alfred A. Knopf, 2006) p. 213.

164 Pat Williams, Jim Denney, *How to Be Like Walt* (Deerfield Beach, FL: HCI, 2004) p. 110.

165 James Collins, Jerry I. Porras, *Built to Last* (New York: Harper Collins, 2002) p. 100-101.

166 Pat Williams, Jim Denney, *How to Be Like Walt* (Deerfield Beach, FL: HCI, 2004) p. 112.

167 Pat Williams, Jim Denney, *How to Be Like Walt* (Deerfield Beach, FL: HCI, 2004) p. 111.

168 James Collins, Jerry I. Porras, *Built to Last* (New York: Harper Collins, 2002) p. 100-101.

169 Pat Williams, Jim Denney, *How to Be Like Walt* (Deerfield Beach, FL: HCI, 2004) p. 116.

170 Pat Williams, Jim Denney, *How to Be Like Walt* (Deerfield Beach, FL: HCI, 2004) p. 120.

171 Retrieved August 11, 2009 from http://www.boxofficemojo.com/alltime/adjusted.htm.

172 Pat Williams, Jim Denney, *How to Be Like Walt* (Deerfield Beach, FL: HCI, 2004) p. 187.

173 Daniel Gross, *Forbes Greatest Business Stories of All Times* (New York: John Wiley & Sons, 1996) p. 137.

174 Neal Gabler, *Walt Disney* (New York: Alfred A. Knopf, 2006) p. 501.

175 Neal Gabler, *Walt Disney* (New York: Alfred A. Knopf, 2006) p. 524.

176 James Collins, Jerry I. Porras, *Built to Last* (New York: Harper Collins, 2002) p. 39.

177 Pat Williams, Jim Denney, *How to Be Like Walt* (Deerfield Beach, FL: HCI, 2004) p. 124.

178 Herb Miller, *Money Is Everything* (Nashville, TN: Discipleship Resources, 1994) p. 19.

179 Vishnu Karmaker and Thomas Whitney, *Mental Mechanics of Archery* (Littleton, CO: Center Vision, Inc., 2006) p. 7.

180 Rich DeVos, Billionaire, Owner of the Orlando Magic.

181 Jon M. Huntsman, Sr., *Business with Integrity* (Provo, UT: Brigham Young University Press, 2005) p. 94.

182 Colin Powell.

183 David J. Schwartz, *The Magic of Thinking Big* (New York: Simon and Schuster, 1959) p. 204.

184 Anthony Robbins, *Unlimited Power* (New York: Fireside, 1997) p. 113–114.

185 Wilbur Wright, Orville Wright, Octave Chanute, and Marvin Wilks McFarland, *The Papers of Wilbur and Orville Wright: 1899-1905* (McGraw-Hill, 1953) p. 75.

186 Stephen M.R. Covey, *The Speed of Trust*, (New York: Free Press, 2006) p. 109.

187 Sam Walton, *Sam Walton* (New York: Doubleday, 1992) p. 30-31.

188 Daniel Gross, *Forbes Greatest Business Stories of All Times* (New York: John Wiley & Sons, 1996) p. 123.

189 Jacob Wassermann, *Columbus, Don Quixote of the Seas* (Boston: Little, Brown and Co., 1930) p. 19–20.

190 William D. Phillips, Jr. and Carla Rahn Phillips, *The Worlds of Christopher Columbus* (New York: Cambridge University Press, 1992) p. 152–153.

191 Anthony Robbins, *Unlimited Power* (New York: Simon & Schuster, 1986) p. 14.

192 Abraham Lincoln, Charles W. Moores (Editor), *Lincoln Addresses and Letters* (New York: American Book Company, 1914.

193 C.S. Lewis, *Mere Christianity* (New York: Simon & Schuster, 1996) p. 166.

194 Henry David Thoreau, *Thoreau's Thoughts* (Boston: Houghton, Mifflin and Company, 1890) p. 11.

195 Alonzo Rothschild, *Honest Abe* (Boston and New York: Houghton Mifflin Company, 1917) p. 222-224.

ILLUSTRATION CREDITS

Graphic Illustrations by Nathan Shirley   **Page #**
Book Cover and Layout

Foundation Commissioned Illustration by Jessica Shirley

Foundation Commissioned Painting by Allison Zeyer

Courtesy of Wal-Mart, Inc.

Public Domain

About the Author

Cameron C. Taylor graduated with honors from the Marriott School of Business and is the author of several books including *Does Your Bag Have Holes? 24 Truths That Lead to Financial and Spiritual Freedom, 8 Attributes of Great Achievers,* and *The Statement of Excellence Workbook.* He is the founder and president of multiple organizations, including the Does Your Bag Have Holes? Foundation. Accomplishments include becoming a published author at age 23, building a multimillion-dollar company by age 27, and establishing a company with over $10 million a year in revenue by age 30. Cameron also serves as a volunteer pastor. He is a recipient of the *Circle of Honor Award* for being an "exceptional example of honor, integrity, and commitment." Cameron lives in the Rocky Mountains with his wife Paula and their three children, Mitchell, Kennedy, and Enoch.

About the Does Your Bag Have Holes? Foundation™

All author proceeds from this book go to the Does Your Bag Have Holes? Foundation. The Foundation is a non-profit educational charity. Its mission is to inspire the world to learn and live the principles of freedom. The Foundation seeks to achieve this mission through publishing books, holding seminars, and providing speakers to businesses, universities, churches, associations, and other organizations. All revenue and donations are used to further the Foundation's mission and for other humanitarian efforts.

Does Your Bag Have Holes? Foundation
428 E. Thunderbird Road #504, Phoenix, AZ 85022
Phone: 1-877-664-6537 • Fax: 1-480-393-4432
Service@DoesYourBagHaveHoles.org
www.DoesYourBagHaveHoles.org

Invite Cameron C. Taylor to Speak

Cameron C. Taylor has presented to organizations all across the country. He would be honored to be a part of one of your meetings. Below are some of his presentations, which he can tailor and adapt to fit your needs.

Title: 8 Attributes of Great Achievers
Summary: Jim Collins, author of *Good to Great*, discovered that the "good-to-great companies placed greater weight on character attributes." This presentation will:

- Help people develop the character attributes which lead to greater productivity and success.
- Help your organization create sustained, superior performance by helping you develop your most valuable resource—your people.
- Inspire, educate, and entertain.

Title: Live Your Dreams: 5 Steps to Goal Achievement
Summary: From this presentation, you will learn:

- Steps to discover and achieve your inspired goals and mission.
- How to become one of the top 3 percent of achievers in the world.
- Powerful stories about those who persisted through failures to achieve their goals.

Title: The 10 Principles and Choices of Prosperity
Summary: Based on the 4 principles and 6 choices presented in the book *Does Your Bag Have Holes?* This engaging and entertaining seminar presents parables, metaphors, and inspiring real life stories that have been developed through years of research.

Other Topics:
Divine-Centered Leadership
How to Succeed with People
The Statement of Excellence Workshop

For more information or to schedule Cameron C. Taylor to speak, call 1-877-664-6537 or send an email to Speaker@DoesYourBagHaveHoles.org

ANOTHER BOOK BY CAMERON C. TAYLOR

DOES YOUR BAG HAVE HOLES?
24 Truths That Lead to Spiritual and Financial Freedom.
ISBN#: 9780979686108, 320 pages with abridged audio book on CD.

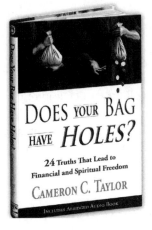

"This is a warm, wonderful book full of timeless truths you can apply to every area of your life."

BRIAN TRACY,
Author of *The Way to Wealth*

"This book contains analogies and short stories that will touch your heart and mind. After reading this book, I see a new potential for myself and others. It is liberating as a Christian to know that business and religion can work hand in hand and that one can be financially independent and spiritually free."

LEE GILLIE, High School Science Teacher

"For over 30 years my company has taught tens of thousands of individuals the keys to financial success coupled with the principles of human happiness. After reading *Does Your Bag Have Holes?* I wish I could have issued it as a core textbook to each and every student of the past three decades."

G. KENT MANGELSON,
President of Wealth of America Training Centers, Ltd.

"Inspiring lessons of truth and wisdom beautifully applied to today's world."

SEAN COVEY, Author of
The Seven Habits of Highly Effective Teens